1953 — 1969

Eisenhower, Kennedy, & Johnson

ROURKE'S COMPLETE HISTORY OF OUR PRESIDENTS ENCYCLOPEDIA

Volume 10

Kelli L. Hicks, Editor

Ypsilanti District Library
5577 Whittaker Road
Ypsilanti, MI 48197

Rourke Publishing

Vero Beach, Florida 32964 | www.rourkepublishing.com

© 2009 Rourke Publishing LLC

All rights reserved. No part of this book may be reproduced or utilized in any form or by any means, electronic or mechanical including photocopying, recording, or by any information storage and retrieval system without permission in writing from the publisher.

www.rourkepublishing.com

PHOTO CREDITS: Pages 4, 26 ©Jason Register; Pages 5, 36, 37 Courtesy of the Lyndon Baines Johnson Library and Museum; Pages 6,10, 20, 31, 50 ©Wikipedia; Pages 8, 15, 18, 34 ©Library of Congress; Page 9 ©alexkon, Israel License (cc-by-sa-2.0), Library of Congress; Pages 12, 13, 14, 16, 17, 21 ©Courtesy of the Dwight D. Eisenhower Presidential Library; Page 19 ©Getty Images; Pages 24, 27, 28, 29, 30, 32, 33 ©Courtesy of the John F. Kennedy Presidential Library; Page 25 LBJ Library photo ©Frank Muto; Pages 38, 41, 42 LBJ Library photo ©Cecil Stoughton; Page 39 LBJ Library photo ©O.J. Rapp; Page 40 LBJ Library photo ©Robert Knudsen; Pages 43, 45, 46, 53 LBJ Library photo ©Yoichi R. Okamoto; Pages 44, 47, 49, 51 LBJ Library photo ©Frank Wolfe; Page 48 LBJ Library photo ©Mike Geissinger.

Editor: Kelli L. Hicks

Cover and interior design by Nicola Stratford, bdpublishing.com

Library of Congress Cataloging-in-Publication Data

Rourke's Complete History of Our Presidents Encyclopedia / Kelli L. Hicks
    p. cm.
Includes bibliographical references and index.
Summary: Discusses the political lives and times of the men who served as United States presidents, their administrations, and the events which occurred during their tenures.
  Set ISBN 978-1-60694-293-2
  Title ISBN 978-1-60694-303-8
  1. Presidents—United States—Juvenile literature.

Printed in the USA
CG/CG

ROURKE PUBLISHING

www.rourkepublishing.com – rourke@rourkepublishing.com
Post Office Box 3328, Vero Beach, FL 32964

America in the 1950s and 1960s 4

Dwight Eisenhower (1953-1961) 10

John F. Kennedy (1961-1963) 22

Lyndon Johnson (1963-1969) 34

Times of Change 50

Cabinet Members 54

Timeline 56

Presidents of the United States 60

Index 62

Further Reading 64

America in the 1950s and 1960s

When President Dwight D. Eisenhower won the presidential election, the 1950s were just getting underway. When President Lyndon B. Johnson left office, the 1960s were just ending. These were two exceptionally lively decades for the United States. Battles over Communism raged at home and abroad, and American society underwent great upheavals.

The changes in world governments that followed World War II (which ended in 1945) shaped the world of the 1950s. Tensions developed between the Soviet Union and its "satellite" republics, those formerly independent countries over which it now had at least some, if not complete, political control on the one side, and the United States and Western European democracies on the other. The situation became known as the Cold War. When the U.S. discovered in 1949 that the Soviet Union had atomic capabilities, these tensions increased dramatically.

The Soviet Union was dissolved on December 8, 1991.

President Lyndon Johnson, at right, listens as Soviet Premier Aleksei Kosygin speaks at the Glassboro Summit Conference in 1967. The two leaders met to discuss Arab-Israeli tensions in the Middle East and U.S.- Soviet arms limitations.

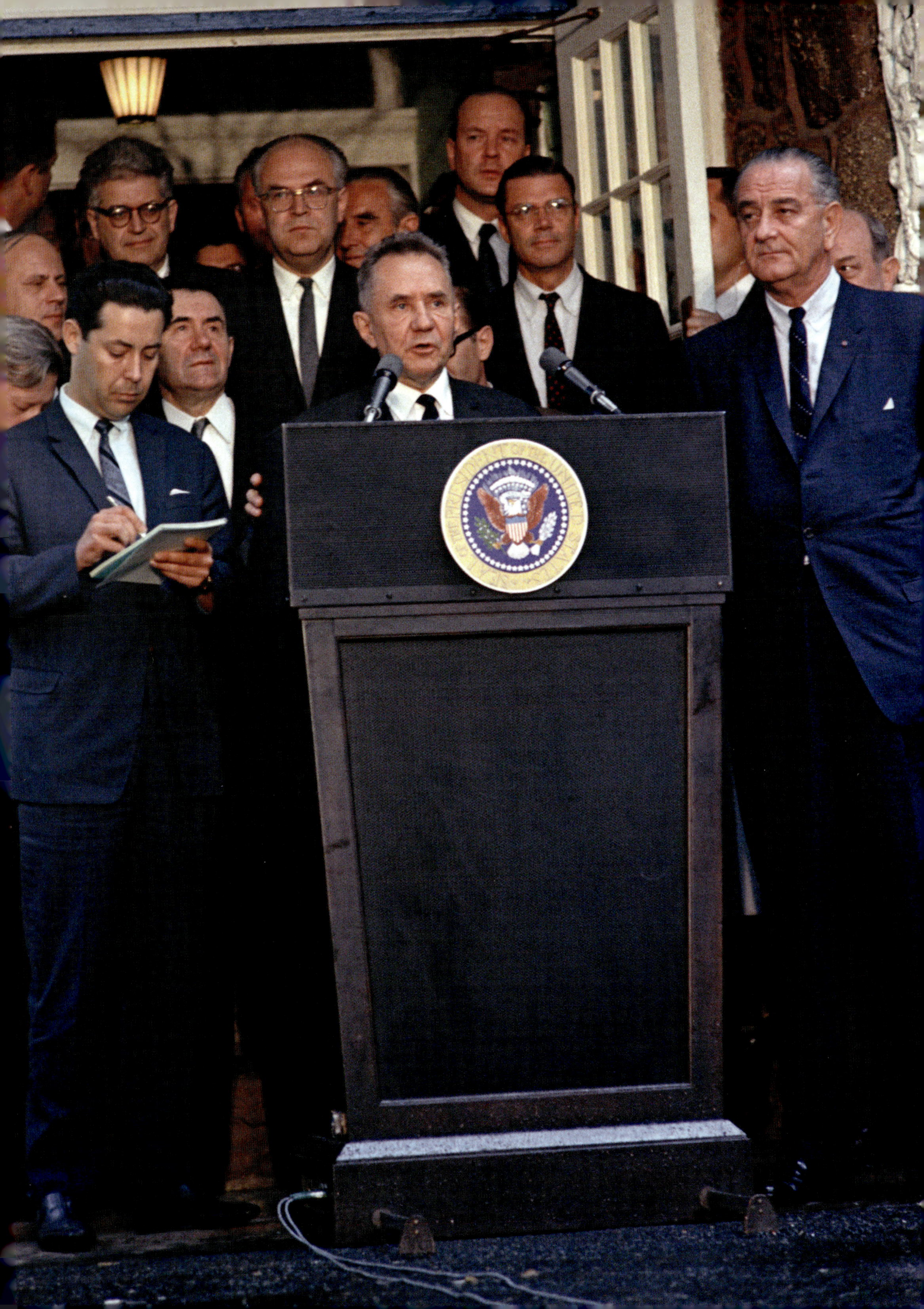

America in the 1950s and 1960s

The mushroom cloud from the atomic bomb dropped on Nagasaki, Japan, rose 11 miles (18 kilometers) into the atmosphere.

The dropping of atom bombs on Japan by the United States in 1945 helped to end World War II and ushered in the atomic age. In 1952, the United States test-exploded a hydrogen bomb (or H-bomb), capable of even greater destruction than the awesome atom bombs. In 1953, word came that the Soviets, too, had developed such a weapon.

Americans asked how the Soviets had been able to develop an atomic weapons program so quickly. Many believed that spies were to blame and that Communists in America, in particular in the U.S. government, were trying to help the Soviets take over the United States. The fact that Communist leaders around the world were gaining control of additional countries bolstered these fears.

In 1949, the Chinese Communists, led by Mao Zedong, used military force to gain control of China. The next year, the Communists of North Korea invaded U.S.-supported South Korea. The United States and other democratic nations contributed troops to a United Nations force that was sent to defend South Korea.

Mao Zedong

A TV Culture

In 1948, there were fewer than 17,000 television sets in the United States. In 1950, there were about 3 million, and by the end of the decade, about 50 million American homes had television sets.

As the average American tuned in more and more, concerns over the increasing use of television became more widespread. Some people warned that television violence would corrupt the morals of the young. Others feared that it would mean the end of books and the fine arts.

I Love Lucy was one of the most-watched series, with other favorites including *Dragnet*, *The Honeymooners*, and *Leave It To Beaver*. Quiz shows became extremely popular, with *What's My Line* being among the most watched. Kids could watch *Lassie*, *The Mickey Mouse Club*, and *Disneyland*. And for those who wanted fine dramatic art, there were such programs as the 1953 televised version of *Hamlet*.

Politicians now used television for their own gain, too. In 1950, Senator Estes Kefauver of Tennessee televised his Special Investigations of Organized Crime, which gave him national fame.

The 1952 presidential nominating conventions were the first such events nationally televised. Here, Americans watched the activities of politicians with amazement and amusement. In his famous "Checkers" speech, vice-presidential candidate Richard Nixon successfully used television to appeal to the American people. He asked that the people keep him on the Republican ticket despite charges of accepting illegal funds.

Although the television medium worked in his favor in 1952, television would be partly responsible for Nixon's failed presidential campaign in 1960. A poor appearance during televised debates with presidential hopeful Senator John F. Kennedy made him look sinister and sickly. Many believe it was this appearance that lost the election for Nixon.

When America's military involvement in Vietnam increased in 1965, TV crews went with the troops. On the nightly news, Americans watched the burning of Vietnamese villages and the transporting of body bags carrying the remains of U.S. servicemen. It was the first war in which non-participants could actually see what was happening on the front lines. By and large, Americans did not like what they were seeing.

As the use of television grew, it had a tremendous impact on American life. The fact that Americans across the country watched the same shows, the same news, and the same commercials contributed greatly to the spread of a common culture.

America in the 1950s and 1960s

In the United States, the House Un-American Activities Committee (HUAC) held hearings on suspected Communist subversives, people trying to destroy the government, and spies. Led by Republican senator Joseph McCarthy, "Red-hunters" ("Red" being a common term for Communist) accused hundreds of Americans of being Communist sympathizers. The careers of many innocent people were ruined when they were accused of having links to the Communist Party, often with little or no proof to back the charges.

Joseph McCarthy served as United States senator from Wisconsin from 1947 until his death in 1957.

Some Americans responded to this "Red Scare" by building bomb shelters to hide in if the Communists attacked the United States. Most Americans, however, just wanted to enjoy the good life of the 1950s, moving to the suburbs to build a house and raise children. They also watched a lot of television. As a consequence of television's growing influence, the most popular programs soon inspired a number of fads. By the end of the decade, for example, there were few middle-class American children who did not own a Davy Crockett coonskin cap or a Mickey Mouse watch.

Not all Americans were eligible to participate in this life of fun and prosperity, however. In most places in the South, segregation, the legalized separation of the races, was enforced. In the North, unwritten gentleman's agreements and other practices kept African Americans out of "white" neighborhoods and schools and out of the best jobs.

Finally, in 1954, a landmark Supreme Court decision known as Brown v. Board of Education of Topeka ruled that segregation in schools was unconstitutional. This paved the way for the nonviolent protest movement that emerged in the years to come. This civil rights movement, led by the Reverend Dr. Martin Luther King, Jr., sought to end all forms of segregation and to make real America's promises of justice and equality.

The civil rights movement led to other social movements in the 1960s, including the peace movement, the ecology movement, and the women's rights movement. In the midst of all this social upheaval, some Americans chose to "turn on, tune in, and drop out."

America in the 1950s and 1960s

A new counterculture of "hippies" developed its own clothes, its own language and music, and its own belief system, including an advocacy of drug use. Long hair, acid rock, marijuana and LSD, long flowing skirts and tattered jeans all were the emblems of the hippies. They were young adults who rejected all that their parents' generation stood for.

Hippies believed in the free expression of peace, love, and non-conformance.

Meanwhile, there were astounding strides in science and technology, ranging from the polio vaccine to the rocket ship. The "race to the moon" spurred advancements in many related fields, including computers, telecommunications, and plastics. And running throughout this period was the ever-increasing political tension between the United States and Communist-centered countries such as East Germany, Cuba, and Vietnam.

Among the many changes occurring during this time period were the advances in space exploration. This included Neil Armstrong's historic walk on the moon on July 21, 1969.

Words to Know

subversives (sub-VURS-ivs): People who try to overthrow or undermine the government.

segregation (seg-ruh-GAY-shuhn): The practice of keeping separate. Historically, the United States has had some laws requiring segregation, or separation, of the races.

gentleman's agreements (JEN-tuhl-muhns uh-GREE-muhnts): Practices in which people agree verbally or with a handshake, as opposed to in writing.

counterculture (KOUN-tur-KUHL-chur): A group of people whose values are different from, and generally opposed to, those of a larger group. In the 1960s, there was a counterculture of young adults who lived in ways very different from the main body of society.

telecommunications (tel-uh-kuh-myoo-nuh-KAY-shuhns): The methods of using electronic impulses to communicate words, pictures, and sound, such as radio, television, and telegraph.

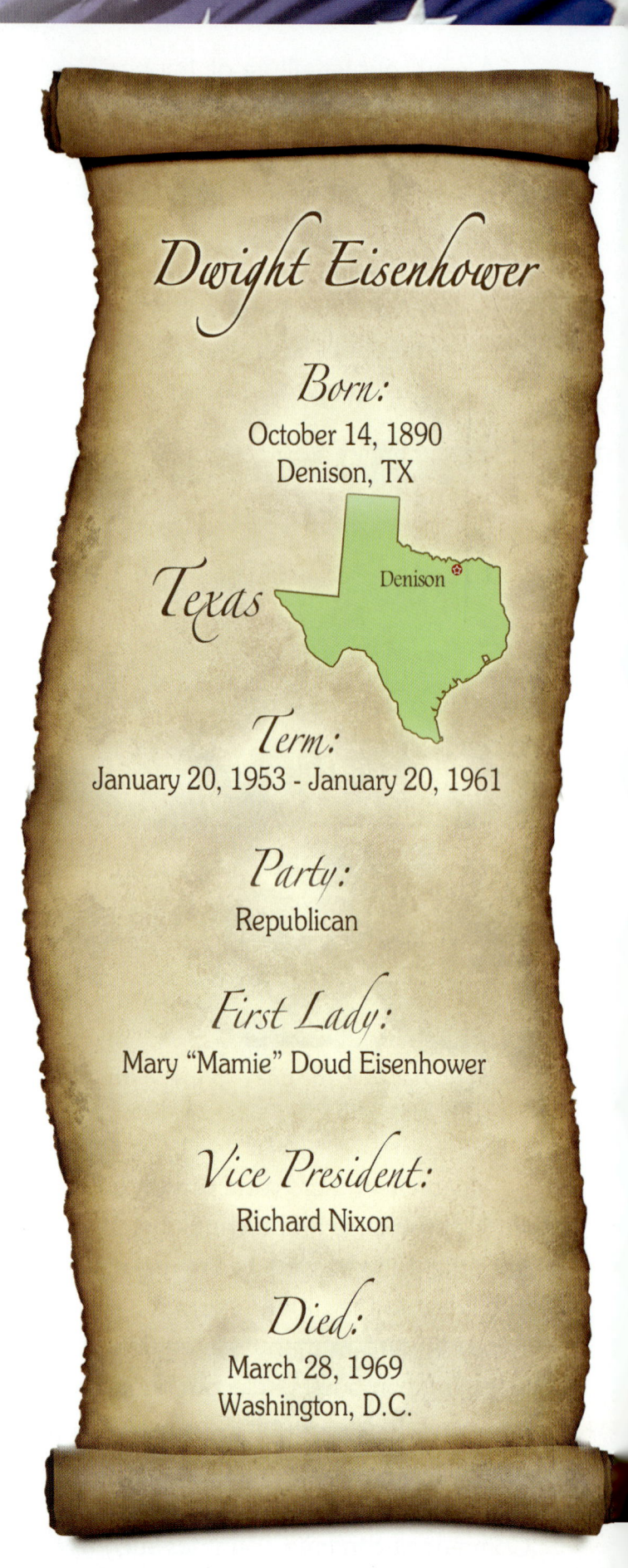

Dwight Eisenhower

In March 1952, President Harry S. Truman announced that he would not run for the presidency again. He had served most of Franklin Roosevelt's fourth term and another four years after his own election in 1948. As the Democrats scrambled to see who would be their presidential candidate, the Republicans chose a war hero, General Dwight David Eisenhower.

From the Wild West to Hero of the Western World

Born in Denison, Texas, on October 14, 1890, Dwight D. Eisenhower moved as an infant to Abilene, Kansas, once a rowdy center of the Wild West. In 1911, he entered the U.S. Military Academy at West Point. During World War I, he trained soldiers. After the war, in 1932, he became an aide to General Douglas MacArthur.

Vice President Richard Nixon

Dwight Eisenhower

Born:
October 14, 1890
Denison, TX

Texas — Denison

Term:
January 20, 1953 - January 20, 1961

Party:
Republican

First Lady:
Mary "Mamie" Doud Eisenhower

Vice President:
Richard Nixon

Died:
March 28, 1969
Washington, D.C.

Dwight Eisenhower

34th President of the United States

Dwight Eisenhower

When the United States entered World War II in 1941, Eisenhower began working with General George Marshall to prepare America's battle plans as part of the Allied effort.

The Allies were the nations including the United States, the Soviet Union, Great Britain, and France, that joined forces to fight the Axis powers, Germany, Italy, and Japan. Eisenhower soon earned the command of the Allied attack on German-occupied North Africa and Europe. In 1943, General Eisenhower, known as "Ike," prepared for Operation Overlord. This was the code name for the invasion of Europe from Britain through France.

Dwight D. Eisenhower

They launched Operation Overlord on June 6, 1944. They called it D-day, from a military term referring to any day on which a crucial operation is to occur. The operation was successful, and the Germans retreated to Germany, where they finally surrendered in May 1945. Later that year, Eisenhower was named army chief of staff, the highest rank in the army.

In 1948, Eisenhower wrote a book about his war experience and accepted the presidency of Columbia University. By 1951, however, he was back in Europe at President Truman's request to help start NATO. NATO, the North Atlantic Treaty Organization, was a mutual-defense organization to help Western Europe and North America defend themselves against aggressors.

During his years in the military, Eisenhower carefully kept himself removed from politics. He was not eager to seek elected office, but both parties approached him about running for president as their candidate. Ike was also unsure of which party he preferred. When he finally decided he was a Republican, the party's leaders worked hard to convince him to accept the 1952 nomination, which he finally did. To help him win the election, Eisenhower chose California senator Richard Nixon as his running mate.

Dwight Eisenhower 13

The Democrats chose Illinois governor Adlai Stevenson as their candidate, with John Sparkman as his running mate. Stevenson attacked the work of Communist-hunting Senator McCarthy, whom he called the "great accuser." Eisenhower, on the other hand, supported McCarthy's reelection bid in Wisconsin. Eisenhower charged that tolerance for Communism poisoned the Truman years.

When Democrats charged that vice-presidential candidate Richard Nixon had accepted illegal financial gifts from supporters, some Republicans called for his removal from the ticket. Nixon went on television to present his case to the American people. He described himself and his family as average Americans with common tastes.

His wife, he said, wore an inexpensive cloth coat, not mink. He said that, yes, there had been some gifts of money, but he had used this money only for his campaign. He admitted that his daughters were given a dog named Checkers as a gift, which they loved. Republicans across the country responded favorably to what they called the Checkers speech, and the next day, Eisenhower told him, "Dick, you're my boy."

Eisenhower and Nixon campaign for the 1952 presidential election.

Dwight Eisenhower

In October 1952, Eisenhower declared that if elected, he would go to Korea to end the war. He claimed that he would do whatever was required to get the job honorably done. This made a tremendous impact on potential voters. His easygoing personality, fatherly mannerisms, and cheerful grin also appealed to Americans.

"I Like Ike" buttons were worn from coast to coast. When they went to the ballot booths in November, American voters gave Ike a landslide victory. Now, the "Hero of the Western World" was president, and there was a Republican in the White House for the first time in 20 years.

The Presidency

The few weeks after the election, even before his official inauguration, Eisenhower fulfilled his promise to go to Korea. He inspected the troops and hinted that the U.S. might use atomic weapons if the Communists did not negotiate for peace.

After the inauguration, however, Eisenhower settled into a somewhat bland presidency. Compared to the activist presidencies of Roosevelt and Truman, who believed that the government should be actively involved in helping Americans, Eisenhower was quite different. He believed in limiting the powers of the presidency.

President Eisenhower picked wealthy businessmen to serve in his cabinet. The one exception was Secretary of Labor Martin Durkin, ex-president of the International Plumber's Union. This led to a joke about Ike's Cabinet being "eight millionaires and a plumber."

Eisenhower's choice of cabinet members was a signal that this administration would be friendlier to business than the Democrats had been. To stimulate business, Eisenhower urged Congress to pass a huge tax-reform bill, which he signed into law in August 1954. During the next two years, more Americans than ever before were able to enter the middle-class.

Dwight D. Eisenhower takes the oath of office on January 20, 1953.

Dwight Eisenhower

First Lady Mamie Eisenhower

Always known by her nickname "Mamie," Mary Geneva Doud was born in Boone, Iowa, on November 14, 1896. When she was a young girl, her family moved to Colorado and later purchased a second home in San Antonio, Texas, where they spent several months of the year. One day in 1915, when Mamie was 18, she and her family visited Fort Sam Houston near San Antonio. That was where she met Lieutenant Dwight D. Eisenhower, whom she married on July 1, 1916.

As an army wife, Mamie had to move many times. In fact, she moved with Ike about 28 times. The eight years that the Eisenhowers lived in the White House were the longest single stay at one address since their marriage.

In 1921, their three-year-old son, Doug Dwight, died of scarlet fever. In 1922, another son, John, was born. John would later follow in his father's footsteps by attending West Point and serving in the army.

As First Lady, Mamie said she did not believe it was her place to interfere in the affairs of government. Her specialty was hospitality, and she was known as a gracious hostess. Whether her guests were the king and queen of Greece, the emperor of Ethiopia, or the premier of the Soviet Union, Mamie made them all feel welcome. She especially enjoyed quiet evenings with her husband, family, and friends.

Like Ike, Mamie had many health problems. She had a weak heart, an ailment that had earlier claimed her sister's life. She also had Ménière's disease, a problem in the inner ear that affected her sense of balance, causing her to sometimes stumble and bump into things.

After the White House years, Mamie was ready to enjoy a more quiet life with Ike. She also looked forward to living in a house of her own.

When Eisenhower was hospitalized in 1968, she was given a nearby room so that she could be by his side almost constantly. She was there when he died.

Mamie lived quietly for another ten years after Dwight's death, until she suffered a stroke in September 1979. She died on November 11, three days shy of her 83rd birthday. Her place of birth has been made into a national museum.

Dwight Eisenhower

Joseph Stalin, political leader of the Soviet Union, died in March 1953, and Eisenhower used the opportunity to try to reduce Cold War tensions and speed up peace negotiations in Korea. Both sides exchanged sick and injured prisoners. On July 27, 1953, they signed a truce that stopped the fighting and left Korea divided between the Communist North and the Democratic South, just about as it had been before the war. It had cost the United States billions of dollars and 54,000 lives.

This limited victory intensified the fears of some that the Communists were taking over the world. Playing on these fears, Senator McCarthy expanded his Red-hunting activities. When McCarthy accused the army of harboring Communists, the nation watched the televised hearings, and most people were disgusted. In December 1954, the U.S. Senate censured, or officially condemned, McCarthy for his behavior, and the era of McCarthyism was over.

Meanwhile, there was trouble brewing in the French colony of Indochina, in Southeast Asia. The French were losing control to Communist forces in the colony and asked the United States to send troops. Eisenhower feared that if Indochina fell to the Communists, other nearby countries would also fall. He described this as the domino theory.

However, he did not send troops to Indochina because he felt the costs would be too great. As a result, the French forces were defeated. Indochina was renamed Vietnam and split in two, with the Communists taking control of the North. In South Vietnam, Eisenhower supported local efforts to fight Communist rebels by sending U.S. financial support and military advisers.

President-elect Dwight D. Eisenhower, third from left, observes field training exercises on a December 1952 trip to Korea.

Dwight Eisenhower 17

There were some who said that the Eisenhower administration was more concerned about freedom in Asia than freedom in America. In December 1955, an African American named Rosa Parks refused to give up her seat on a bus to a white man, as local laws required in Montgomery, Alabama.

When police arrested Rosa, the African American community organized a boycott, a refusal to use the city's buses. For more than a year, they peacefully protested this form of racial segregation until the U.S. Supreme Court declared the laws illegal in November 1956.

Eisenhower was cautious about civil rights. He thought that the Supreme Court's decisions against segregation might create more problems than they solved. As the president, however, he said that it was his duty to uphold the law of the land.

Heart Attack and Reelection

President Eisenhower loved to play golf. On September 24, 1955, after a long day on the links, he had a heart attack and they rushed him to the hospital. While he lay in bed recovering, Vice President Nixon and other administration officials carried on the work of the government. In November and December, Eisenhower gradually returned to work.

By February 1956, he announced that he would be available to run for reelection. He did his best to look energetic and fit as he campaigned on television and in person.

On February 29, 1956, Eisenhower announced that he would seek a second term in office.

Words to Know

McCarthyism (muh-KAHR-thee-iz-uhm): The belief in and support of Senator Joseph McCarthy in his publicly accusing people of acts of disloyalty and relation to the Communist Party, on the basis of little or no actual evidence.

18   Dwight Eisenhower

Despite his health problems, Ike remained an immensely popular president, and his party renominated him. Although some Republicans urged Eisenhower to dump Nixon, the vice president remained his running mate. The Democrats chose Adlai Stevenson again. A young Massachusetts senator named John F. Kennedy made a bid for the vice-presidential nomination, but instead corruption-fighter Estes Kefauver got the nomination.

In October, an international crisis erupted when Egypt took control of the Suez Canal. Then, just a few days before the U.S. presidential election, Soviet tanks rumbled through the streets of Budapest, Hungary, crushing a rebellion against the Communist government. With these problems, Americans decided that the man who had led the Allies to victory was the best man to have in the White House. Ike won his second term easily.

The Second Term

Soon after his second term began, Eisenhower asked Congress for funds and military forces to aid any nations "requesting assistance against armed aggression from any country controlled by . . . Communism." This became known as the Eisenhower Doctrine.

Domestic controversies, however, erupted before international ones did. In 1957, Eisenhower signed a Civil Rights Act. It created a Civil Rights Commission, which would investigate the practices that kept many African Americans from being able to vote.

The South was not going to accept without a fight what it considered to be federal interference in states' affairs. In defiance of the Supreme Court ruling to end school segregation, Governor Orval Faubus of Arkansas called out the state's National Guard in September 1957.

Words to Know

federal (FED-ur-uhl): Having to do with the national government, as opposed to state or local governments.

In the 1954 Supreme Court case Brown v. Board of Education, the Court ruled "separate educational facilities are inherently unequal." The landmark decision paved the way for integrated classrooms such as this one at Anacostia High School in Washington, D.C.

The Polio Vaccine

One of the most terrifying diseases of the early 1950s was poliomyelitis, commonly known as polio. Polio is a contagious disease caused by several viruses. By 1950, approximately 34,000 people were afflicted with it each year in the United States. It was most common among children, often leaving them crippled. Sometimes polio victims experienced such severe paralysis that they had to lie in a machine called an "iron lung" in order to breathe.

In the late 1940s, a research physician named Jonas Salk was studying viruses such as the ones that caused polio. His hope was to create a vaccine to fight the disease. Vaccines worked by injecting a small amount of the disease-causing virus into a healthy person. This prompts the person's body to create antibodies to fight the disease. Once the person builds up antibodies, he or she is generally immune to the illness.

In 1952, one of the worst polio epidemics ever afflicted nearly 60,000 Americans. Fortunately, by March 1953, Dr. Salk had produced what he thought might be a safe and effective vaccine. It was ready for the final test: It had to be tried on people and in particular, it had to be given to children.

Salk began to give the vaccine to small groups of children under carefully controlled conditions. In 1954, about 1,830,000 school children voluntarily participated in a study that took nearly a year to evaluate. At the end of that time, the evaluators were able to declare that the vaccine worked.

President Eisenhower asked the secretary of Health, Education, and Welfare to come up with a plan to distribute the vaccine. Over the next few years, many children received immunizations, and the number of cases of polio in the United States began to decline dramatically. Today, polio has practically disappeared in the United States, with only a handful of cases reported each year.

As for Jonas Salk, he returned to the laboratory to perfect his vaccine and to go on to investigate the relationship between cancer and the immune system. In the 1980s, he became involved in efforts to find a vaccine for AIDS. His work incomplete, he died on June 23, 1995, in California.

Dr. Jonas Salk

Dwight Eisenhower

His goal was to keep nine African American students from entering Little Rock's Central High, a school that had only white students. President Eisenhower demanded that Faubus obey the Supreme Court ruling. The threat of violence was so extreme that the president had to send an army unit to Little Rock to accompany the nine students to school.

Three weeks after Governor Faubus blocked the students' entry into the all-white school, soldiers from the 101st Airborne Division escort the Little Rock Nine students into Central High School on September 25, 1957.

As soon as the Little Rock situation was under control, Eisenhower had a new problem to worry about. On October 4, 1957, the Soviets sent a satellite, called Sputnik, into space. Many Americans were horrified to think that the Soviets were ahead of the United States in science and technology. They feared that this indicated Soviet superiority in military capabilities as well. In July 1958, the National Aeronautics and Space Administration (NASA) was officially created. Its goal was to put America in the space race.

While some people focused on the moon, others had concerns closer to home. The Eisenhower Doctrine was tested in Lebanon in July 1958, when the president sent troops there at the request of that country's government. The president did not send troops to Cuba, however, when a Communist leader, Fidel Castro, won control of that country early in 1959.

In the spring of 1960, an American plane was shot down over the Soviet Union and its pilot captured. The United States felt great embarrassment by the incident. They first denied that the plane was on a spy mission, and then admitted that it was. As Eisenhower completed his term and prepared to leave the presidency, peace, one of his major goals, seemed to be threatened.

After the White House

Eisenhower was the first president required by law to leave the White House after completing two terms. The 22nd Amendment to the Constitution passed in 1951, limited the president to two presidential terms. Eisenhower moved to his farm in Pennsylvania and took an active interest in raising animals and pursuing other hobbies.

Dwight Eisenhower

In retirement, he wrote three books: *The White House Years: Mandate for Change* (1965); *Waging Peace* (1966); and *At Ease: Stories I Tell to Friends* (1967). Even out of the White House, he remained one of the most popular men in America.

In March 1968, Eisenhower entered the hospital to receive treatment for his failing health. He died on April 28, 1969. At the time, his former vice president, Richard Nixon, was president. At Ike's funeral service, Nixon revealed some of the former president's last words to America: "I've always loved my wife. I've always loved my children. I've always loved my grandchildren. I've always loved my country."

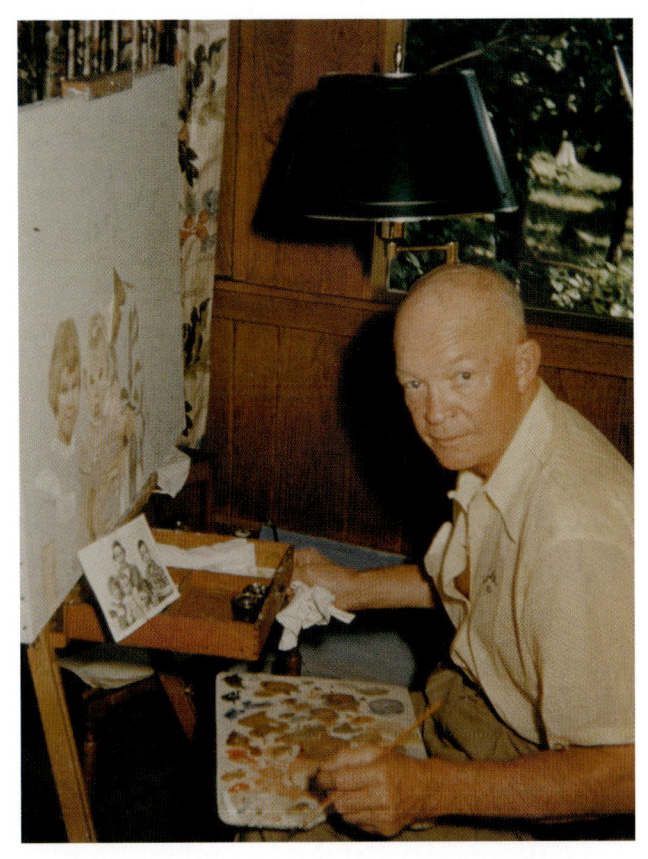

Painting was just one of Eisenhower's hobbies.

President Nixon places a wreath on the casket of Dwight D. Eisenhower.

John F. Kennedy

When President Eisenhower handed over the reins of power to John F. Kennedy, he was the oldest president ever to leave the White House. At the same time, he turned over the government to the youngest president ever elected. As a result of the so called baby boom that followed World War II, more Americans than ever before were under the age of 30.

Somehow it seemed appropriate for the nation to have a young and handsome president. Eventually, some would compare his term in office to the time of Camelot, the mythical and romantic kingdom of the legendary King Arthur, who took power at an early age.

Vice President Lyndon Johnson

John F. Kennedy

Born:
May 29, 1917
Brookline, MA

Massachusetts
Brookline

Term:
January 20, 1961 - November 22, 1963

Party:
Democratic

First Lady:
Jacqueline Bouvier Kennedy

Vice President:
Lyndon Johnson

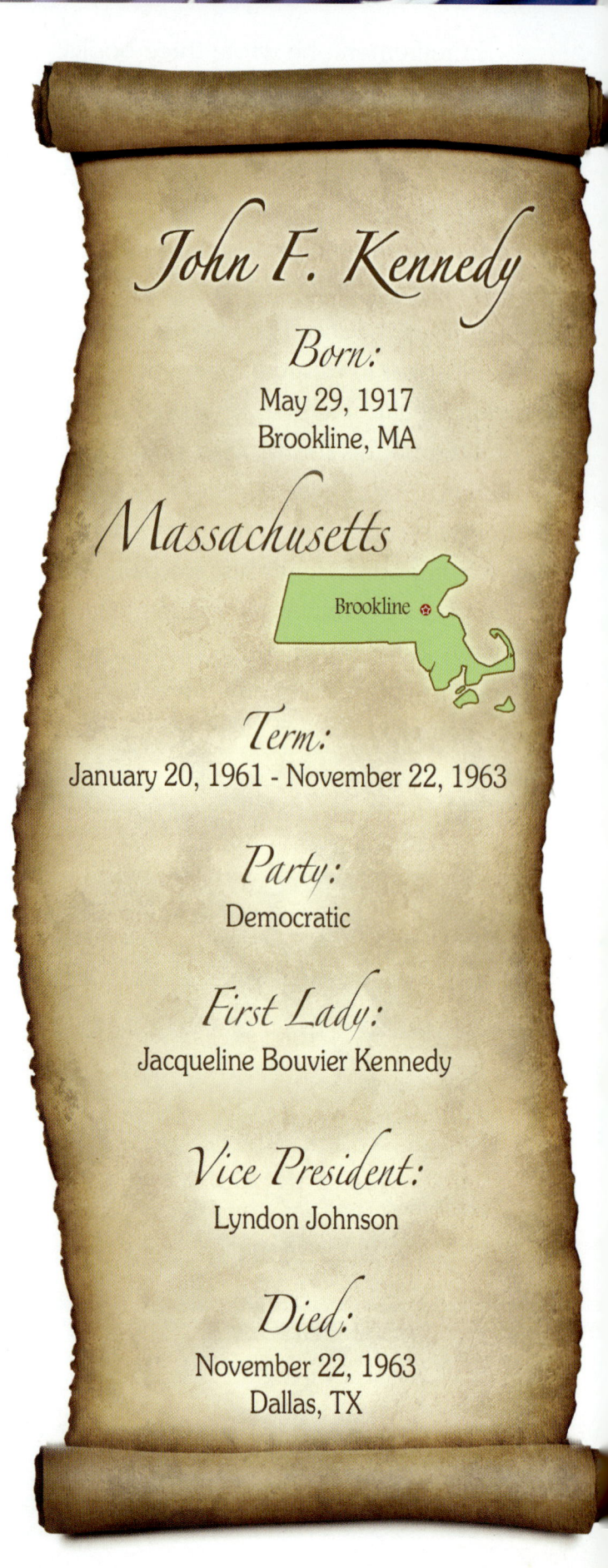

Died:
November 22, 1963
Dallas, TX

John F. Kennedy

35th President of the United States

John F. Kennedy

Kennedy's Early Career

John "Jack" Fitzgerald Kennedy was born on May 29, 1917, in Brookline, Massachusetts. The son of self-made millionaire Joseph Kennedy and grandson of Boston politician "Honey" Fitzgerald, the boy was born into a family that enjoyed power.

Jack graduated from Harvard University in 1940 after studying government and international relations. In 1941, he enlisted in the navy. During World War II, he commanded a PT (patrol torpedo) boat in the South Pacific. One night, a Japanese destroyer cut the ship in two. Kennedy and ten other survivors swam for four hours to reach an island from which they were rescued a few days later. Kennedy later received the Purple Heart for his leadership and heroism.

Lieutenant John F. Kennedy sits aboard the PT-109 in the South Pacific, 1943.

In 1946, he held his first elected office, winning a seat in the U.S. House of Representatives for Massachusetts. In 1952, he took on the popular and respected Henry Cabot Lodge for a Senate seat. Although Republican presidential candidate Dwight Eisenhower won big in Massachusetts that year, Democrat Kennedy defeated Republican Lodge for the Senate seat.

In 1953, Kennedy married a society debutant and newspaper reporter, Jacqueline Bouvier. From that moment on, their romance would be the center of great public fascination.

Between October 1954 and February 1955, Kennedy underwent several operations on his back, which he injured in the war. While recovering, he wrote a book called *Profiles in Courage* (1956), which described difficult moral choices made by great senators. It won him a 1957 Pulitzer Prize.

In 1956, the Democratic National Convention chose Adlai Stevenson to run against Dwight Eisenhower for the second time. Senator Kennedy made the important speech nominating Stevenson at the convention. He came close to being Stevenson's running mate, but the party chose Estes Kefauver instead. In the end, Republicans Eisenhower and Nixon won the election.

From that time on, however, Kennedy began preparing to run for the presidency himself. In 1958, he won reelection to the Senate. He then began entering political contests called primaries in a number of states.

His closest competitor was Hubert H. Humphrey, Democratic senator from Minnesota. Kennedy's victories in the primaries bolstered his claims that he could win the presidential election, despite his Roman Catholic religion, which some people saw as a major disadvantage. There had been no Roman Catholic previously elected president. Some people were afraid that a Catholic president would be too influenced by the leader of the Catholic Church, the pope.

When the Democrats held their nominating convention, another name that they considered was that of Senator Lyndon B. Johnson of Texas. Johnson had not entered the primaries, hoping that at the convention they might choose him as a compromise candidate. But the Kennedy-backers had worked hard to line up the votes they needed, and Kennedy won on the first ballot.

Johnson was named vice-presidential candidate to help Kennedy in the South, where it was feared Kennedy's religion and his northeast liberal background would hurt him. In his acceptance speech at the convention, Kennedy looked to a future with lots of work to do. He called it a "new frontier," but he warned that "the new frontier of which I speak is not a set of promises—it is a set of challenges."

In September 1960, Senators Kennedy and Johnson campaigned in Austin, Texas.

John F. Kennedy

The Republicans nominated Richard Nixon as their presidential candidate, with Henry Cabot Lodge as his running mate. Many of the experts predicted that Nixon would win. Nixon hoped that he would benefit from President Eisenhower's popularity and a reputation as a hard-liner against communism.

Both Nixon and Kennedy were ambitious young men who conducted vigorous campaigns. Nixon claimed to have more experience than Kennedy, while Kennedy criticized Nixon's principles. Both candidates traveled from one end of the country to the other, shaking hands and making speeches. Kennedy, however, had a great personal charm and charisma. His speeches were clever and witty, and many people responded favorably to his boyish good looks and friendly smile.

In September and October 1960, the two candidates met for a series of four debates. Although presidential debates had been part of the American political process for a long time, this was the first time they were nationally televised. And that made all the difference. Nixon, who was not feeling well, looked tired and sick, while Kennedy looked fresh and tanned. People who listened to the debates on the radio thought that Nixon was the stronger candidate, but people who watched on television favored Kennedy. His ability to recite many facts and figures from memory was particularly impressive.

When Election Day came, Kennedy received almost 120,000 more popular votes than Nixon (out of nearly 69 million votes), and in the Electoral College, he had 303 votes to Nixon's 219. This made him the victor. While Kennedy waited to be sworn in as president, he and his wife were also awaiting the birth of a baby. Their son, John F. Kennedy, Jr., was born a few weeks after Election Day, joining three-year-old sister Caroline in the president-elect's family.

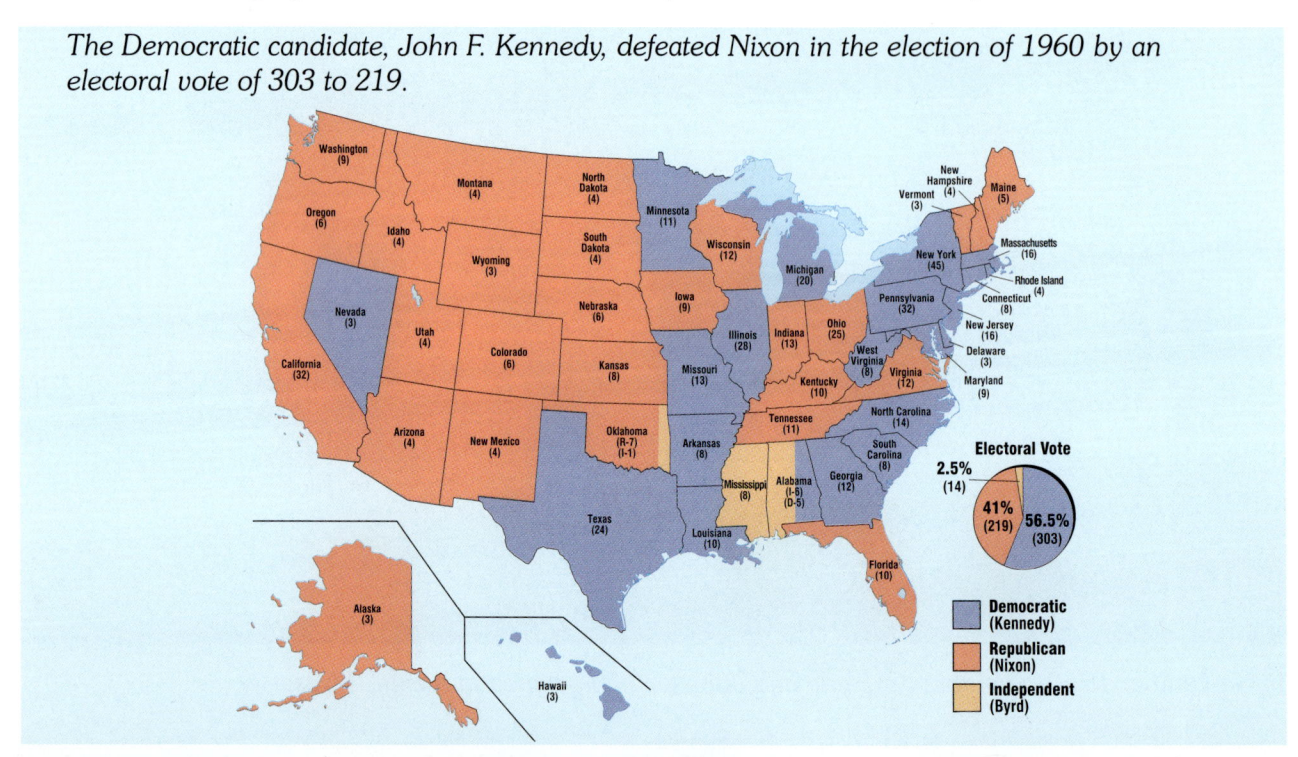

The Democratic candidate, John F. Kennedy, defeated Nixon in the election of 1960 by an electoral vote of 303 to 219.

First Lady Jacqueline Bouvier Kennedy

Jacqueline Lee Bouvier was born on July 28, 1929, in Southampton, New York. She loved to ride horses and frequently appeared in horse shows from the age of five on. Growing up, she attended some of the world's most prestigious schools, including the Sorbonne in Paris, France.

Jacqueline was working for a newspaper in 1951 when she met a young senator from Massachusetts named Jack Kennedy. He was 36 years old and she was 24 when they married on September 12, 1953. Daughter Caroline was born four years later, on November 27, 1957. Three years after that, Jacqueline was pregnant while her husband conducted his presidential campaign. Their son, John, Jr., was born November 25, 1960, just a few weeks after Kennedy won the presidential election.

"Jackie," as her husband and many others called her (although she preferred Jacqueline), was admired as a strikingly beautiful First Lady. Women around the country copied her clothes, hats, and the way she wore her hair.

Jackie was also a very intelligent, independent, and capable woman. She was a dedicated supporter of the arts and of historical preservation. She took on the job of restoring the White House, furnishing it with authentic American antiques. When she finished the job, she gave a televised tour to the American people.

In spring of 1963, the Kennedys announced that they expected a third child. Unfortunately, Patrick Bouvier Kennedy was born several weeks premature in August and died two days later. Jackie was still recovering from this loss, and beginning to help her husband with the 1964 reelection campaign, when he was shot to death in a Dallas, Texas motorcade as she sat beside him. The dignity with which she conducted herself in the hours and days after her husband's death greatly comforted the American people.

For a long time afterward, Jacqueline dedicated herself to preserving her husband's memory. Then, in October 1968, amid much public criticism, she married wealthy Greek businessman Aristotle Onassis. In 1975, Onassis died and made her a widow for the second time. She later returned to work in journalism, editing books for a major publisher in New York City. The entire nation, which never lost its fascination for this charming and brave woman, grieved with fond remembrance in May 1994, when Jacqueline Kennedy Onassis died of cancer.

John F. Kennedy

The "New Frontier"

On January 20, 1961, Kennedy delivered one of the nation's most memorable inaugural speeches. "The torch has been passed to a new generation of Americans," he said. "Ask not what your country can do for you: Ask what you can do for your country." In that speech, the new president outlined some of the programs of his "new frontier."

Military units pass the reviewing stand at the inaugural parade for President Kennedy.

One of the most popular and successful of the new programs was the Peace Corps. It was a program to send thousands of American volunteers, mostly college-age youths, into all the corners of the world, where they would help people in a variety of ways. Some would dig ditches for irrigation systems. Others would teach children to read. Still others would immunize people against disease.

Considering space the ultimate "new frontier," Kennedy also supported expansion of the space program. On May 25, 1961, speaking before Congress, he declared, "I believe that this nation should commit itself to achieving the goal, before the decade is out, of landing a man on the moon and returning him safely to earth."

Despite early successes on the domestic front, Kennedy got off to a rocky start in the area of foreign affairs. On April 17, 1961, Cuban exiles living in Florida landed in Cuba, at the Bay of Pigs, with the assistance of the U.S. government. They planned to lead a revolution against Communist leader Fidel Castro. But Castro's forces were waiting for them, and they quickly captured the invaders.

It was a humiliating experience for America and for the new president, who accepted full responsibility for the defeat, even though the prior administration actually planned the attack.

The president's prestige was somewhat restored a few weeks later when he and his wife traveled to Europe. Jacqueline Kennedy was so popular with the French that President Kennedy said, upon his return, "I am the man who accompanied Jacqueline Kennedy to Paris, and I have enjoyed it."

Words to Know

blockade (blok-ADE): The use of ships or other forces to block off an area.

John F. Kennedy

The Kennedys also met with Soviet premier Nikita Khrushchev and his wife in Vienna, Austria. Again, Mrs. Kennedy got much attention. However, things did not go well between President Kennedy and Premier Khrushchev. Tensions were building over control of the city of Berlin in East Germany.

A few months later, in August 1961, the Russians built a wall on their side of the divide between East and West Berlin. This wall prevented East Berliners from leaving the Communist-controlled sector of the city. The Berlin Wall remained a source of tension for the next 28 years. On November 9, 1989, crossing points between East and West Berlin opened. When government officials began dismantling the wall, thousands of people joyfully assisted them.

During his 1963 visit to West Berlin, President Kennedy inspects the Berlin Wall.

On October 23, 1962, President Kennedy signs a proclamation to prevent the arrival of any more shipments of Soviet military weapons in Cuba.

One of the most dramatic face-offs between East and West took place in October 1962. Photographs taken from the air showed the installation of Soviet nuclear missiles in Cuba. President Kennedy announced that the United States would blockade the coast of Cuba to prevent Soviet ships from delivering materials necessary to complete the missile installations.

John F. Kennedy

The world held its breath as Soviet ships headed toward the blockade. Americans stood on alert, waiting to see what would happen next. If the Soviets provoked a fight, it could have been the beginning of World War III or even a nuclear holocaust. Luckily, the Soviet ships turned back. In return for a U.S. promise not to invade Cuba, the Soviets withdrew the missile installations.

During Kennedy's administration, U.S. involvement in South Vietnam increased. More military advisers went to the area, as tensions grew increasingly worse. These were not combat troops; they were advisers sent to train the South Vietnamese Army. There had been a few hundred U.S. personnel there in 1960.

By late 1963, there were more than 16,000. When South Vietnam's ruthless president Ngo Dinh Diem was assassinated in November 1963, Kennedy and his advisers hoped that a more tolerant leader would be elected. Unfortunately, this would not be the case.

Meanwhile, there were plenty of problems at home. African American civil rights leaders were demanding more support from the federal government to end segregation and other injustices. On August 28, 1963, the March on Washington attracted some 200,000 peaceful protesters who demonstrated in the capital for jobs and freedom. Afterward, several of the protest leaders, including Martin Luther King, Jr., met with President Kennedy, who vowed to support a new civil rights act.

When Kennedy learned that the Soviets had renewed their testing of atomic weapons in the atmosphere, he began underground tests. In April 1962, the United States began testing over the Pacific Ocean.

In July 1963, the United States, along with Great Britain and the Soviet Union, agreed to a treaty banning atmospheric, outer space, and underwater testing of nuclear weapons. This Nuclear Test-Ban Treaty was considered one of the greatest accomplishments of the Kennedy administration, and the president planned to use it in his upcoming reelection bid.

Words to Know

boycott (BOI-kot): To refrain from buying products, paying for services, or dealing with certain people as a form of protest.

sit-ins (SIT-INZ): A method of protest in which people sit down and refuse to move until certain demands are met.

President Kennedy addresses the nation on Civil Rights.

The Civil Rights Movement

After the U.S. Supreme Court's 1954 Brown v. Board of Education of Topeka decision, African Americans gained some hope. It seemed that at last they would begin to receive the equal treatment they were entitled to under the Constitution.

The success of the Montgomery Bus Boycott in 1956 inspired individuals such as Reverend Martin Luther King, Jr., to take further action. He created the Southern Christian Leadership Conference (SCLC) to organize the civil rights cause. The National Association for the Advancement of Colored People (NAACP) also participated, helping African Americans fight for their constitutionally guaranteed rights.

Martin Luther King Jr., gives a lecture on March 26, 1964.

As the 1960s began, grassroots civil rights protests spread spontaneously across the nation. From lunch counters to libraries, swimming pools, and public parks throughout the South, citizens conducted a variety of peaceful protests such as "sit-ins," "read-ins," and "wade-ins," to show that segregation must go.

Some protests were impromptu reactions to random incidents. Others were carefully orchestrated and well planned by national organizations. The Congress of Racial Equality (CORE) conducted "Freedom Rides" in 1961 to protest segregation on interstate buses and in their terminals. Many of the protesters received brutal beatings by angry mobs, but the protests continued.

In June 1963, President Kennedy sent a civil rights bill to Congress. "It ought to be possible for Americans of any color to receive equal service in places of public accommodation, without being forced to demonstrate in the street," he said. Two months later, 200,000 people participated in the March on Washington, demanding that the government take action.

In the shadow of the Lincoln Memorial, they gathered to listen to speeches by a number of people, including Reverend King, who spoke of his dream that some day black and white children in America could play and learn and grow up together in peace and harmony. On that day, he promised, all Americans would be able to say, "Great God Almighty, we are free at last."

Tragedy in Dallas

As Kennedy prepared for the campaign of 1964, he decided to visit a number of places that would be important for his reelection. One of these was Texas. Despite warnings that there were those in Dallas who hated him, he went there on November 22, 1963, accompanied by his wife.

As he rode from the airport in an open car, he waved to the crowds that lined the streets. The governor of Texas, John Connally, was riding in the car just in front of the Kennedys and was happy with the response the president was getting. Then, at about 12:30 in the afternoon, several shots rang out. President Kennedy slumped forward in his seat with blood spattered around him. A Secret Service agent jumped on top of him, and the car raced to the nearest hospital. At about 1:00 p.m. doctors declared John F. Kennedy dead.

The sudden, violent death of the young president shocked the nation. About 250,000 people, young and old, rich and poor, Republicans and Democrats, passed by his flag-draped coffin in the Capitol Rotunda to pay their respects. On television, Americans saw the president's widow and children kneel before the coffin. Representatives from 102 nations attended the funeral.

Three-year-old John F. Kennedy, Jr., saluted as his father's coffin passed, pulled by a riderless horse. Mrs. Kennedy lit an eternal flame at the president's gravesite in Arlington National Cemetery. To many, Kennedy's assassination marked the end of America's innocence.

President and Mrs. Kennedy disembark Air Force One at Love Field, Dallas, Texas on November 22, 1963.

John F. Kennedy

Lee Harvey Oswald was an employee at the Texas Book Depository, the building from which the shots seemed to have originated. Police arrested Oswald in Dallas on the day of the shooting and charged him with the assassination. Two days later, Jack Ruby, a nightclub owner, shot and killed Oswald during live national television coverage as police transferred Oswald from one jail to another.

Lyndon Johnson, who was sworn in as president one and a half hours after Kennedy died, appointed a committee to investigate the assassination. People suggested many theories. There were rumors that Cuba's Fidel Castro had been behind it. Other theories suggested it was the leaders of organized crime who had contracted for the president's death.

Led by Chief Justice of the Supreme Court Earl Warren, the investigating committee became known as the Warren Commission. They called its findings the Warren Report. The Warren Report concluded that Oswald acted alone in shooting the president. But debate about the assassination continues to this day, and many questions remain unanswered.

President Kennedy's body lies in state in the East Room of the White House, November 23, 1963.

Lyndon Johnson

All his life Lyndon Johnson had been saying "I'm going to be president of the United States someday." But when he took the oath of office aboard the presidential plane, Air Force One, it was not the way he had expected it to be. Everyone around him was in shock or in tears, and John F. Kennedy's coffin was only a few yards away.

The Early Years

Lyndon Baines Johnson was born in the Pedernales Valley of Texas on August 27, 1908. He grew up in the town of Johnson City, named for his grandfather, Sam Ealy Johnson, Sr. Lyndon's father Sam Ealy Johnson, Jr., was a member of the Texas state legislature for six terms.

Vice President Hubert H. Humphrey, Jr.

Lyndon Johnson

Born:
August 27, 1908
Stonewall, TX

Texas

Term:
November 22, 1963 - January 20, 1969

Party:
Democratic

First Lady:
Claudia "Lady Bird" Taylor Johnson

Vice President:
Hubert H. Humphrey, Jr.

Died:
January 22, 1973
San Antonio, TX

Lyndon Johnson

36th President of the United States

Lyndon Johnson

This photo of Lyndon Johnson, taken around 1927, dates from his years as a teacher.

More successful in politics than business, the family was very poor during much of Lyndon's youth. The young man worked hard, however, and graduated from Southwest Texas State Teachers College in 1930, during the Great Depression. He got a job teaching public speaking at a small high school and coached the debate team to 66 victories in 67 attempts.

He got his first job in Washington, D.C., in 1931 as personal secretary to Texas congressman Richard Kleberg. In November 1934, Johnson married Claudia Taylor, known best by her nickname "Lady Bird." Soon afterward, he received the appointment to the National Youth Administration (NYA) director for Texas by President Franklin D. Roosevelt. In 1937, Johnson campaigned for and won the seat of a congressman from Texas who had died.

When the United States declared war on Japan on December 8, 1941, Johnson, who had been in the U.S. Naval Reserve, requested active duty. In June 1942, while assessing U.S. military strength in the Pacific for President Roosevelt, the B-26 plane he was aboard was attacked by Japanese fighter planes. Only with great difficulty did the crew manage to get back to base. For his participation in the ordeal, Johnson was later awarded the Silver Star.

Lyndon Johnson was a member of the Southwest Texas State Teachers College Debate Team.

Lyndon Johnson

In 1948, he ran for the Senate and won a very narrow victory. Johnson knew how to get legislation passed, and he went to work immediately doing just that. He put in extraordinarily long hours "wheeling and dealing" and giving people the "Johnson treatment."

This was Johnson's technique: He would put his face up close to the person he was talking to, speaking fast and forcefully, sometimes with obscenities. He might also put his arm around and poke the person to make his point.

Very quickly, he became the Democratic Party whip, the powerful figure that sees to it that senators are present when it is time to vote and that they know how the party wants them to vote. In 1953, he was voted the minority leader in the Senate.

When the Democrats gained control of the Senate in 1955, Johnson became Senate majority leader. This made him one of the most powerful men in the country, along with President Eisenhower and Speaker of the House of Representatives Sam Rayburn.

Although Eisenhower was a Republican and Rayburn and Johnson were Democrats, the three men respected one another and worked well together. Johnson was instrumental in getting bills passed that the president wanted and, in return, getting the president to accept some of the measures that the Democrats wanted.

Johnson constantly put in long hours in his office, although a heart attack in 1955 forced him to slow down a little. He worked hard for the passage of the Civil Rights Act of 1957. He managed to convince southern Democrats who were against it that it could be worse, and northern liberals, who wanted a stronger bill, that it was better than nothing. In 1960, Johnson also helped to pass a voting rights bill, which further strengthened the Civil Rights Act.

Lyndon Johnson addressed crowds from his helicopter during his 1948 campaign for the Texas Senate.

Lyndon Johnson

"Stepping Down" to Be Vice President

As a number of Democrats began campaigns for the presidency in 1960, Lyndon Johnson was definitely interested. Many people believed that he had proven himself capable during his years in the Senate, but they also thought that it would be difficult for a southerner to win the presidential election. As it turned out, candidate John F. Kennedy came to the convention with enough votes earned during the primaries to win the nomination easily.

Johnson had little in common with the young senator from Massachusetts. That was exactly why some party leaders suggested that Kennedy should ask Johnson to be his running mate. They felt Johnson would balance the ticket and give it strength in the South, where Kennedy was weak. In fact, Johnson did help Kennedy win in Texas, a key state in what turned out to be a very close election.

The experience of the vice-presidency was not very pleasant for Johnson. He was used to being a man with power, and the vice president has very little of that. In the minutes after Kennedy was shot on November 22, 1963, Secret Service agents moved to protect Vice President Johnson, realizing probably before anyone else that he would now be president. He waited in a darkened room in the hospital while doctors tried to save Kennedy's life. When Kennedy was pronounced dead, Johnson was driven in an unmarked police car to the presidential plane. Within two hours of Kennedy's death, Lyndon Johnson, with his wife, Lady Bird, on one side and Kennedy's widow, Jacqueline, on the other, took the oath of office as the 36th president of the United States.

Lyndon Johnson is sworn into office aboard Air Force One on November 22, 1963.

Carrying on the Kennedy Plans

President Johnson rose magnificently to the challenge of taking over the presidency. When he got off the plane in Washington, D.C., he delivered his first official words as president: "This is a sad time for all people. We have suffered a loss that cannot be weighed. . . . I will do my best. This is all I can do. I ask for your help—and God's."

At a joint session of Congress a few days after the funeral, Johnson reminded people that Kennedy had said "Let us begin." Now, Johnson added, "Let us continue." In asking Congress to swiftly pass a civil rights law, Johnson said, "We have talked long enough in this country about equal rights. We have talked for 100 years or more. It is time now to write the next chapter, and to write it in the books of law." He signed into law the Civil Rights Act of 1964.

President Johnson signs the Civil Rights Act of 1964.

Lyndon Johnson

First Lady Claudia "Lady Bird" Johnson

Claudia Alta Taylor was born on December 22, 1912, in Karnack, Texas. One of the family servants said that she was as pretty "as a lady bird," and the name stuck. Lady Bird's mother died when she was five, so her Aunt Effie moved in to help raise the little girl. Lady Bird graduated from the University of Texas with a degree in liberal arts and journalism.

She met Lyndon B. Johnson while he was visiting the office of a friend one day late in the summer of 1934. He took her for a ride in his car and told her that he wanted to marry her. Within two months, he had convinced her, and they were married on November 17, 1934. Throughout their marriage, she would be both her husband's business partner and political partner.

She borrowed from her future inheritance to help finance Lyndon's 1937 race for Congress. She kept the congressional office running while he was serving in World War II. In 1942, she purchased a nearly bankrupt radio station in Austin, Texas. Within a few years' time, it had become a multimillion-dollar broadcasting empire called Texas Broadcasting Corporation.

The Johnsons had two daughters. Lynda Bird was born on March 19, 1944, and Lucy Baines, who later changed her name to Luci, was born on July 2, 1947. All the Johnsons thus had the initials LBJ.

When her husband was vice president, Lady Bird especially enjoyed the roll of hostess for many events. When he was running for the presidency in 1964, she also learned to enjoy campaigning. Reporters appreciated her friendliness and her humorous southern expressions such as, "I'll see you Saturday if the Lord be willin' and the creek don't rise".

After the election, she involved herself in her husband's "war on poverty," becoming the national chairperson of the antipoverty program Head Start. When she heard her husband make a speech about the environment, she said, "That's for me" and took up a beautification project to improve both urban and rural America.

Flowers were planted, neighborhoods were cleaned up, and teenagers were given jobs to help. Lady Bird traveled across the country to raise funds and generate interest in the project, and she urged Congress to pass the Highway Beautification Act of 1965. She was one of the most active First Ladies since Eleanor Roosevelt, although she avoided controversial political issues.

On August 6, 1966, Luci Johnson married Patrick Nugent and had her reception in the White House. On June 21, 1967, she gave birth to a son, Patrick Lyndon "Lyn", the president and First Lady's first grandchild. On December 9 of that year, Lynda married Chuck Robb in a White House wedding. She was the first president's daughter to be married in the White House in 53 years. In March, with Lynda expecting a baby in the fall, Chuck left for Vietnam.

The war intruded on the First Lady's work, too, as antiwar protesters hounded her almost wherever she went.

Lady Bird was happy to retire to the LBJ Ranch after their stressful years in the White House. After Lyndon's death, she continued to manage her business interests and, in 1988, published a book, *Wildflowers Across America*. She had been a pioneer in getting environmental concerns put on the national agenda.

President Lyndon B. Johnson gives the State of the Union address in the Capitol Building.

It was even stronger than the civil rights law that Kennedy had asked for. It banned discrimination in most public places and encouraged school desegregation by allowing the federal government to withhold funds from any states, institutions, agencies, and companies that practiced discrimination.

In addition, Johnson trimmed the budget, the amount of money that the government planned to spend, for 1964 so that he could ask Congress for a tax reduction for the American people. He was intent on declaring a "war on poverty," as he said in his State of the Union address in January 1964.

Lyndon Johnson

Later that year, he would say, "Every night when I go to bed, I ask myself: 'What did we do today that we can point to for generations to come, to say that we laid the foundation for a better and more peaceful and more prosperous world?'"

A number of crises threatened President Johnson's ideals in the spring of 1964. There was unrest in Panama, an American plane was shot down over East Germany, and an American-supported government was overthrown in South Vietnam. Some said of Johnson that he was unable "to tame the world as he had tamed Congress."

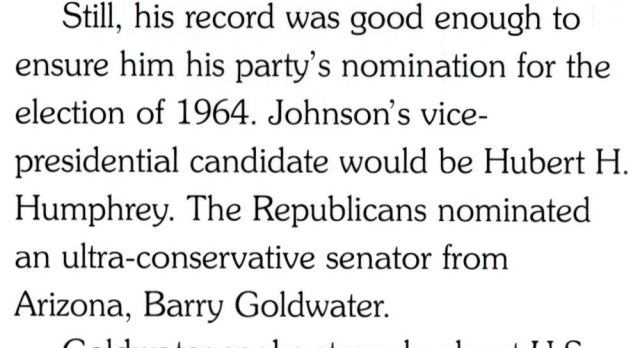

Still, his record was good enough to ensure him his party's nomination for the election of 1964. Johnson's vice-presidential candidate would be Hubert H. Humphrey. The Republicans nominated an ultra-conservative senator from Arizona, Barry Goldwater.

Goldwater spoke strongly about U.S. military might too strongly for many people. Remarks about nuclear weapons such as "Let's lob one into the men's room at the Kremlin [the Soviet capitol]" made it easy for Democrats to portray him as a warmonger. His running mate was William Miller, a little-known congressman from New York.

On August 2, 1964, the Maddox, an American destroyer, was attacked off the coast of North Vietnam in the Gulf of Tonkin. Investigations would later suggest that the United States may have provoked the attack, but the American people did not know that at this time. President Johnson pledged to "meet force with force," and Congress passed the Gulf of Tonkin Resolution.

Lyndon Johnson campaigns in Cleveland, Ohio, for the 1964 presidential race.

Vice President Hubert H. Humphrey, Jr.

Hubert Horatio Humphrey, Jr., was born in Wallace, South Dakota, on May 27, 1911. From 1949 until 1965, he served the state of Minnesota as a U.S. senator. Humphrey gained a reputation as an open-minded and fair man. He worked hard for civil rights legislation. In 1960, he made a bid for the presidency but a lack of funds greatly handicapped him, especially compared to the amount of money that John F. Kennedy had to spend.

Humphrey continued to serve in the Senate during the presidencies of Kennedy and Johnson. He helped to pass the Civil Rights Bill in 1964. It was partly in recognition of this that Johnson chose him to be his vice president. Humphrey seldom questioned the president's decisions and became an outspoken supporter of the U.S. war efforts in Vietnam.

This would later hurt his own chances to be president; he ran unsuccessfully in 1968. Humphrey, who was unable to win the Democratic presidential nomination in 1972, died in 1978. Historians remember him as one of the most respected political figures in Minnesota and the nation.

Words to Know

warmonger (WOR-muhng-ur): A person who advocates or speaks in favor of war.

It allowed the president to take "all necessary measures to repel any armed attack against the forces of the United States and to prevent further aggression." But throughout the rest of the campaign, Johnson promised not to let our "American boys" do the fighting for "Asian boys."

The presidential campaign raised questions about Johnson's morality. There were tales about wild activities on his Texas ranch, his making a small fortune while in the Senate, and his obscene stories. But, these were countered by fear that the "war hungry" Goldwater was worse. When Election Day came, Johnson received 43 million votes to Goldwater's 27 million. Democrats also gained stronger control in both houses of Congress.

The "Great Society"

During the campaign, Johnson had begun to speak of his dreams for a "Great Society." He said, "We have the opportunity to move not only toward the rich society and the powerful society, but upward to the Great Society. The Great Society rests on abundance of liberty for all. It demands an end to poverty and racial injustice." Although he was now wealthy, Lyndon Johnson was one man who did not forget what it was like to be poor.

Early in his full-term presidency, he began to get some of his Great Society programs started, including Job Corps, which helped train poor and disadvantaged people to get better jobs; Head Start, which helped children from underprivileged backgrounds get ready for and do better in school; and Medicare, which provided financial assistance for older citizens in need of medical care.

The Voting Rights Act of 1965 was another achievement for which Johnson fought. "It's not just [blacks], but really it's all of us who must overcome the crippling legacy of bigotry and injustice," he told Congress. "And we shall overcome," he added, using the words of a song that was popular with civil rights activists.

President Lyndon B. Johnson delivers remarks at the signing ceremony for the 1965 Voting Rights Act.

Lyndon Johnson

Johnson, himself, led the way by appointing the first African American Supreme Court justice, Thurgood Marshall, in 1967. But some civil rights leaders, notably Martin Luther King, Jr., began to fear that increasing U.S. involvement in Vietnam was draining attention and resources away from the battle against poverty and discrimination. They were right. The war in Vietnam would soon overshadow all other problems.

Vietnam

Despite Johnson's campaign promise not to send "American boys" to do the fighting for "Asian boys," that is exactly what happened. The number of Americans fighting in Vietnam eventually exceeded half a million, and the troops sent in by Johnson, unlike those of his predecessors, were combat soldiers. This also meant that there would be more U.S. casualties.

In 1961 and 1962, a total of 32 American lives were lost; in 1963, casualties totaled 76; and in 1964, with increased U.S. involvement, the American death toll rose to 136. From 1965 to 1969—during Johnson's full elected term—the American death toll climbed to more than 57,000, and battle injuries mounted to well over 300,000.

After the French left Vietnam, the North Vietnamese continued to train and supply South Vietnamese Communists, known as Vietcong. The Vietcong fought a guerrilla war in South Vietnam, infiltrating the cities and hiding in the rice paddies and the jungle. They had a considerable number of followers among Vietnamese peasants, who had seen little but corrupt governments under democratic regimes. Millions of other Vietnamese did not care who governed them so long as they left them alone.

President and Mrs. Johnson visit with injured servicemen returned from Vietnam.

Lyndon Johnson

During a 1966 visit to Vietnam, President Lyndon B. Johnson awards the Distinguished Service Cross to First Lieutenant Marty A. Hammer.

In February 1965, the Vietcong scored a victory against an American air base at Pleiku in South Vietnam. In response, the United States bombed North Vietnam, in an attack code-named Rolling Thunder.

Thousand of marines, the first actual American combat troops, protected the South Vietnamese bases from which the bombing missions would be flown. During the years that followed, the United States dropped an incredible number of bombs on North Vietnam and on places in South Vietnam believed to be harboring Vietcong.

As the casualties continued to rise, Johnson kept insisting that things were going well, that the Vietcong and North Vietnamese losses were greater than American losses, and that the enemy was on the verge of collapse. Then, on January 30, 1968, during the Vietnamese New Year known as Tet, the Vietcong and North Vietnamese attacked cities throughout South Vietnam, including Saigon, the capital. The success of this attack was proof that the U.S.-supported nation of South Vietnam was not, in fact, winning the war.

Many Americans were outraged at the ever widening "credibility gap," which was the term used for the difference between what Americans were told about the war in Vietnam and what was really happening on the battlefields.

The Antiwar Movement

As the number of American youths dying in Vietnam increased, so did opposition to the war. College campuses held teach-ins to educate people about Southeast Asia and what was happening there. As Americans watched the burning of Vietnamese villages and the evacuation of wounded Americans on the nightly news, they began to turn against what many called "the president's dirty little war."

Young people at home were aghast at the fact that U.S. soldiers were fighting and dying to preserve the South Vietnamese regime, a ruthless and corrupt government. When it was reported on numerous occasions that American soldiers were killing innocent Vietnamese men, women, and children, sentiment began to turn against the American servicemen themselves.

Large and small cities and college campuses held huge demonstrations, which often turned violent. Senator Robert F. Kennedy of Massachusetts, brother of John F. Kennedy, called it "the greatest domestic crisis since the war between the states."

Opposition to President Johnson and his policies grew with every day that passed. In preparation for the 1968 election, antiwar Senators Eugene McCarthy and Robert Kennedy were challenging the president within his own party.

Johnson could not admit that his Vietnam policies had been wrong. This, he felt, would be saying that all the dead servicemen had died in vain. He could also see that he would not win if he ran again and Lyndon Johnson could not bear to lose.

Anti-war protesters gather to listen to speeches at the reflecting pool in Washington, D.C., during the 1967 March on the Pentagon.

48 Lyndon Johnson

Therefore, on March 31, 1968, he announced that he was ending the bombing of North Vietnam and that, to end "the divisiveness among us," he would not run for president again. "I shall not seek, and I will not accept, the nomination of my party for another term as your president," he said.

But it was too late to end the divisiveness and violence. On April 4, 1968, civil rights leader Martin Luther King, Jr., was shot to death outside a hotel in Memphis, Tennessee. Destructive riots broke out across the nation, one of the worst being right in Washington, D.C.

Then, on June 5, as Robert Kennedy celebrated his victory in the California presidential primary, he was shot. He died the next morning. A few months later, the Democratic National Convention, held in Chicago in August, became the scene of more violence and unrest.

Secretary Clark Clifford and another staff member react to the news of Martin Luther King Jr.'s assassination.

Words to Know

primary (PRYE-MAIR-ee): Part of the political election process in which the members of a political party indicate the candidate they wish to nominate for an office.

Inside the convention building, with joyful celebration, Vice President Hubert Humphrey received the nomination for president. But, what Americans saw happening outside the building, an ugly demonstration of unruly protest and police brutality, reflected badly on the Democrats. President Johnson did not even attend the convention for fear of making a bad situation worse.

After the White House

When the emotional 1968 presidential election was finally over, the Republican candidate, Richard Nixon, won the election. Lyndon and Lady Bird Johnson retired to their ranch in Texas. They planned and built a huge presidential library and an addition to the University of Texas. Johnson devoted himself to the running of the ranch, working on the irrigation system and the introduction of new breeds of livestock.

The White House years had not been easy ones for him. By the time he left office at age 60, he had a number of health problems, including a weakened heart.

Johnson died of a heart attack on January 22, 1973. President Nixon was just beginning his second term amid allegations of illegal campaign activities. And, in addition to the news of Johnson's death, newspaper headlines finally proclaimed the long-awaited ceasefire in Vietnam.

President Lyndon B. Johnson pauses for a portrait at the LBJ Ranch near Stonewall, Texas.

Times of Change

American society changed a great deal from the time Dwight D. Eisenhower became president to the time Lyndon B. Johnson left the White House. The pursuit of prosperity, contentment, and conformity characterized the 1950s. The early 1960s were considered energetic, hopeful, and somewhat innocent.

The murder of President John F. Kennedy by an assassin's bullet in 1963 severely shook the nation's sense of innocence. What innocence remained was lost in the rest of the 1960s, with urban riots and the assassinations of Martin Luther King, Jr., and Robert F. Kennedy.

The decade ended with the United States losing a war that had divided the American people like no war had since the Civil War of the 1860s. In 1952, Americans had been chanting "I Like Ike." By 1969, the shouts had changed to "Hey, hey, LBJ, how many kids did you kill today?"

During the Vietnam War, F-105 Thunderchiefs and an EB-66 Destroyer drop bombs on North Vietnam.

Eisenhower was one of the most-loved presidents in the modern era. He was in the White House during a time when the American people wanted a president who would stay out of their business and their pleasure, and that is pretty much what he did.

The presidency of John Kennedy is harder to assess because it was cut so short. During his brief time in the White House, he brought an increased energy and commitment to the Oval Office. Although his actual achievements fell short of his aspirations, he was a president who had great vision and inspired hope.

Some commentators have said that Kennedy was the last president Americans believed in. A poll taken in 1979 found that a majority considered him one of the greatest presidents ever. In more recent years, there have been some criticisms of his personal behavior and his handling of certain foreign crises.

If Kennedy won the election to serve a second term, which most likely would have occurred, it is difficult to know if he would have continued to increase U.S. involvement in Vietnam or moved toward withdrawal. Arguments can be made both ways.

Veterans for Peace protest the Vietnam War at a 19 march on the Pentagon.

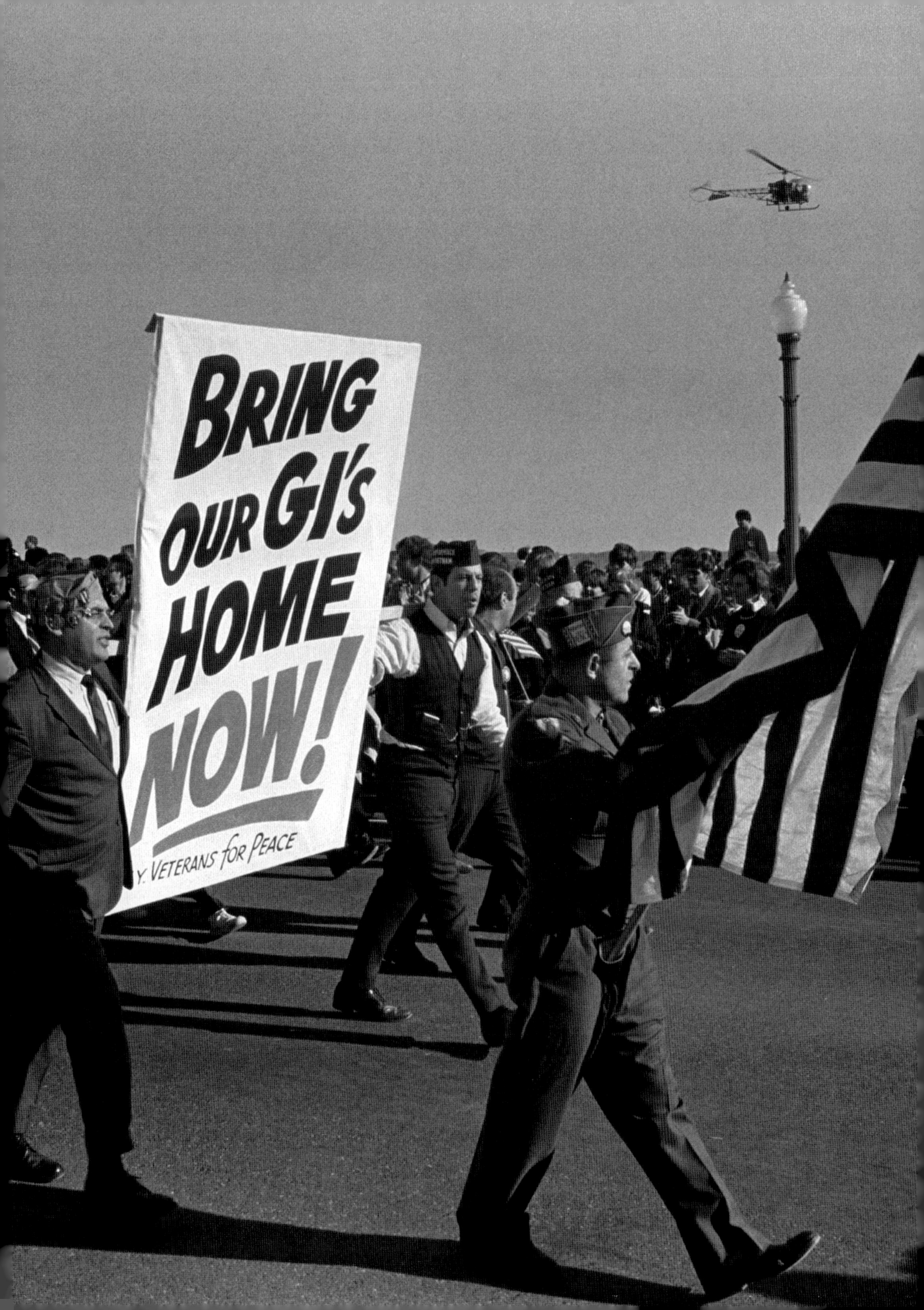
BRING OUR GI's HOME NOW!
Y. VETERANS for PEACE

The Space Race

When Americans learned that the Soviet Union had put the first satellite, Sputnik I, in space in October 1957, they were stunned. Did this achievement in science and technology mean that the Soviets were an even greater military threat than had been thought?

Less than a month later, the Soviets launched Sputnik II. Instead of a small steel ball (Sputnik I had been about the size of a basketball), this spacecraft was 12 feet (3.66 meters) long and cone shaped. It also carried a passenger, a female dog named Laika. Laika spent seven days in orbit, during which Soviet scientists learned a great deal about the effects of space travel on a living creature.

Then, on January 31, 1958, the United States was finally able to enter the space race by sending its first satellite into space. It was a long narrow tube called Explorer I. It went higher than either of the Soviet satellites had and discovered a layer of deadly radiation 600 miles (965 kilometers) above the Earth. Scientists later built special shields to protect humans inside the craft from the dangerous radiation.

On April 12, 1961, the Soviets sent cosmonaut (the Russian word for Astronaut) Yuri Gagarin into space, and after one complete orbit of the Earth, he safely returned to Earth. In May, President John Kennedy challenged America to land a man on the Moon by the end of the decade, but no American had yet left the planet's atmosphere, and most Americans failed to take the president's goal seriously.

The first American in space was Alan Shepard, who spent about 15 minutes in space on May 5, 1961. Not until February 20, 1962, did an American orbit the Earth, when John Glenn accomplished this aboard Mercury 6.

On March 18, 1965, cosmonaut Alexei Leonov became the first human being to go outside of a spaceship and float in space. On June 3 of the same year, American astronaut Ed White accomplished this feat. The Americans were catching up. Then, on December 15, 1965, the Americans moved ahead with a first. Two *Gemini* spacecraft, each traveling 18,000 miles (28,968 kilometers) per hour, moved to within 100 feet (30.48 meters) of each other in space. On March 16, 1966, one American craft actually docked with another in space.

On January 27, 1967, three American astronauts died in a fire in a space capsule during testing. This tragedy horrified the nation and was a setback for the program. But after an investigation and safety improvements, the race was on again. It appeared that the soviets experienced similar tragedies during this time period, but they were not as open with information as the Americans.

Times of Change 53

America's Apollo 8 successfully orbited the Moon and then returned to Earth in December 1968. Apollo 9 tested the disconnecting of a lunar module, the part of the spacecraft designed to land on the Moon, from the main spacecraft and then the reconnection of it. On May 18, 1969, Apollo 10 took the lunar module to within nine miles of the Moon's surface.

On July 20, 1969, Americans listened to the voice of astronaut Neil Armstrong report from space that "the Eagle has landed." The American lunar module was on the Moon. And then, a television camera mounted on the outside of the module began sending pictures back to Earth as Neil Armstrong backed out of the module and became the first person to walk on the Moon. "That's one small step for man, one giant leap for mankind," he said. America had won the race to the Moon and had managed to do it, as President Kennedy had challenged, before the end of the decade.

As for Lyndon Johnson, he was a strong activist president during a period that required forceful leadership. But all the hopes he raised in 1964 and 1965 turned sour as the conflict in Vietnam escalated. By 1968, many Americans felt betrayed.

The mandate they had given Johnson in the landslide election of 1964 was not intended to support a war in Southeast Asia. The fact remains, however, that Johnson took a stronger stand for civil rights than any other president before him, and the changes he helped to bring about in society made a great and positive difference in the quality of American life.

President Lyndon B. Johnson meets with Civil Rights activists the White House in 1965.

Cabinet Members

Eisenhower

VICE PRESIDENT
Richard Nixon

SECRETARY OF STATE
John Foster Dulles
Christian A. Herter

SECRETARY OF THE TREASURY
George M. Humphrey
Robert B. Anderson

SECRETARY OF DEFENSE
Charles E. Wilson
Neil H. McElroy
Thomas S. Gates, Jr.

ATTORNEY GENERAL
Herbert Brownell, Jr.
William P. Rogers

POSTMASTER GENERAL
Arthur E. Summerfield

SECRETARY OF THE INTERIOR
Douglas McKay
Frederick A. Seaton

SECRETARY OF AGRICULTURE
Ezra Taft Benson

SECRETARY OF COMMERCE
Sinclair Weeks
Lewis L. Strauss1
Frederick H. Mueller

SECRETARY OF HEALTH, EDUCATION,
AND WELFARE
Oveta Culp Hobby
Marion B. Folsom
Arthur S. Flemming

SECRETARY OF LABOR
Martin P. Durkin
James P. Mitchell

Kennedy

VICE PRESIDENT
Lyndon B. Johnson

SECRETARY OF STATE
Dean Rusk

SECRETARY OF THE TREASURY
C. Douglas Dillon

SECRETARY OF DEFENSE
Robert S. McNamara

ATTORNEY GENERAL
Robert F. Kennedy

POSTMASTER GENERAL
J. Edward Day
John A. Gronouski

SECRETARY OF THE INTERIOR
Stewart L. Udall

SECRETARY OF AGRICULTURE
Orville L. Freeman

SECRETARY OF COMMERCE
Luther H. Hodges

SECRETARY OF LABOR
Arthur J. Goldberg
W. Willard Wirtz

SECRETARY OF HEALTH, EDUCATION,
AND WELFARE
Abraham A. Ribicoff
Anthony J. Celebrezze

Cabinet Members

Johnson

VICE PRESIDENT
Hubert Humphrey

SECRETARY OF STATE
Dean Rusk

SECRETARY OF THE TREASURY
C. Douglas Dillon
Henry H. Fowler
Joseph W. Barr

SECRETARY OF DEFENSE
Robert S. McNamara
Clark M. Clifford

ATTORNEY GENERAL
Robert F. Kennedy
Nicholas de B. Katzenbach
Ramsey Clark

POSTMASTER GENERAL
John A. Gronouski
Lawrence F. O'Brien
W. Marvin Watson

SECRETARY OF THE INTERIOR
Stewart L. Udall

SECRETARY OF AGRICULTURE
Orville L. Freeman

SECRETARY OF COMMERCE
Luther H. Hodges
John T. Connor
A. B. Trowbridge
C. R. Smith

SECRETARY OF LABOR
W. Willard Wirtz

SECRETARY OF HEALTH, EDUCATION,
AND WELFARE
Anthony J. Celebrezze
John W. Gardner
Wilbur J. Cohen

SECRETARY OF HOUSING AND URBAN
DEVELOPMENT
Robert C. Weaver
Robert C. Wood

SECRETARY OF TRANSPORTATION
Alan S. Boyd

Timeline

1770

1774 — First Continental Congress

1775 — American Revolution begins

1776 — America declares independence from Great Britain

1780

1783 — Treaty of Paris formally ends American Revolution

1787 — U.S. Constitution is written

1789 — George Washington becomes president

1790

1791 — Bill of Rights becomes part of Constitution

1793 — Eli Whitney invents cotton gin

1797 — John Adams becomes president

1800

1800 — Washington, D.C., becomes permanent U.S. capital

1801 — Thomas Jefferson becomes president

1803 — Louisiana Purchase almost doubles size of the United States

1808 — Slave trade ends

1809 — James Madison becomes president

1810

1812 — War of 1812 begins

1814 — British burn Washington, D.C. War of 1812 fighting ends

1815 — Treaty of Ghent officially ends War of 1812

1817 — James Monroe becomes president

1820

1820 — Missouri Compromise is passed

1823 — Monroe Doctrine is issued

1825 — John Quincy Adams becomes president

1828 — Popular votes used for first time to help elect a president

1829 — Andrew Jackson becomes president

Timeline

1830

- **1830** Congress passes Indian Removal Act
- **1832** Samuel Morse has idea for telegraph
- **1835** Samuel Colt patents revolver
- **1837** Martin Van Buren becomes president
- **1838** Native Americans are forced to move to Oklahoma traveling Trail of Tears

1840

- **1841** William Henry Harrison becomes president; John Tyler becomes president
- **1845** James Polk becomes president
- **1845** Texas is annexed to United States
- **1846** Mexican War begins; Boundary between Canada and United States is decided
- **1848** Gold is discovered in California; First women's rights convention is held
- **1849** Zachary Taylor becomes president

1850

- **1850** Millard Fillmore becomes president
- **1850** Compromise of 1850 is passed
- **1853** Franklin Pierce becomes president
- **1857** James Buchanan becomes president

1860

- **1860** Southern states begin to secede from Union
- **1861** Abraham Lincoln becomes president
- **1863** Abraham Lincoln gives Gettysburg Address
- **1865** Andrew Johnson becomes president
- **1865** Civil War ends; Freedman's Bureau is created; 13th Amendment abolishes slavery
- **1868** Impeachment charges are brought against President Johnson
- **1869** Ulysses S. Grant becomes president

1870

- **1873** U.S. economy collapses; depression begins
- **1876** Alexander Graham Bell invents telephone
- **1877** Rutherford B. Hayes becomes president
- **1879** Thomas Edison invents lightbulb

1880

- **1881** James Garfield becomes president; Chester Arthur becomes president
- **1882** Chinese Exclusion Act restricts number of Chinese immigrants allowed into United States
- **1885** Grover Cleveland becomes president
- **1889** Benjamin Harrison becomes president

Timeline

1890

- **1890** U.S. troops kill more than 200 Sioux and Cheyenne at Wounded Knee
- **1893** Grover Cleveland becomes president again
- **1893** Charles and J. Frank Duryea construct first car in the United States
- **1897** William McKinley becomes president
- **1898** Spanish-American War occurs

1900

- **1901** Theodore Roosevelt becomes president
- **1903** Orville and Wilbur Wright fly their plane at Kitty Hawk, North Carolina
- **1908** Henry Ford produces Model T
- **1909** William H. Taft becomes president

1910

- **1913** Woodrow Wilson becomes president
- **1914** Panama Canal opens
- **1917** America enters World War I
- **1919** World War I ends

1920

- **1920** 19th Amendment gives women right to vote
- **1921** Warren Harding becomes president
- **1923** Calvin Coolidge becomes president
- **1927** Charles Lindbergh makes first nonstop flight across Atlantic
- **1929** Herbert Hoover becomes president
- **1929** Stock market crashes; America enters economic depression

1930

- **1933** Franklin D. Roosevelt becomes president
- **1939** World War II begins

1940

- **1941** Pearl Harbor is bombed; America enters World War II
- **1945** Harry S. Truman becomes president
- **1945** United States drops atomic bombs on Hiroshima and Nagasaki; World War II ends; United Nations is formed

Timeline

1950

- **1950** Korean War begins
- **1953** Dwight Eisenhower becomes president
- **1953** Korean War ends
- **1954** Supreme Court orders desegregation of schools
- **1957** Soviet Union launches *Sputnik I*
- **1958** United States launches *Explorer I*; NASA is created

1960

- **1961** John F. Kennedy becomes president
- **1962** Cuban Missile Crisis
- **1963** Lyndon Johnson becomes president
- **1964** Civil Rights Act of 1964 is passed
- **1965** First U.S. troops sent to Vietnam War
- **1968** Martin Luther King, Jr. is assassinated
- **1969** Richard Nixon becomes president
- **1969** Neil Armstrong is first person to walk on moon

1970

- **1970** First Earth Day is celebrated
- **1973** OPEC places oil embargo resulting in fuel shortages
- **1974** Nixon is first president to resign
- **1974** Gerald Ford becomes president
- **1975** War in Vietnam ends
- **1976** America celebrates its bicentennial
- **1977** Jimmy Carter becomes president
- **1978** Leaders of Israel and Egypt sign the Camp David Accords
- **1979** U.S. embassy in Iran is attacked and hostages are taken

1980

- **1981** Ronald Reagan becomes president
- **1981** American hostages are released; Reagan appoints first woman to Supreme Court, Sandra Day O'Connor
- **1986** U.S. space shuttle *Challenger* explodes after lift-off
- **1989** George H. W. Bush becomes president

1990

- **1991** Persian Gulf War occurs
- **1992** U.S. troops are sent to Somalia to lead multinational relief force; Riots explode in Los Angeles
- **1993** William J. Clinton becomes president
- **1993** World Trade Center is bombed by terrorists
- **1995** Bomb destroys federal building in Oklahoma City
- **1998** U.S. bombs Iraq; Impeachment charges are brought against President Clinton
- **1999** First balanced budget in 30 years is passed; Impeachment trial ends

2000

- **2000** Clinton sets aside land for national parks and monuments; Outcome of the presidential race is clouded due to voting miscounts
- **2001** George W. Bush becomes president
- **2001** Terrorist Attack on the World Trade Center; President Bush announces War on Terrorism
- **2002** No Child Left Behind Act is signed into law
- **2003** U.S. troops are sent to Iraq
- **2009** Barack Obama becomes president

Presidents of the United States

President	Birth	Party	Term	Death
George Washington	February 22, 1732; Westmoreland Cty., VA	None	April 30, 1789 - March 4, 1797	December 14, 1799; Mt. Vernon, VA
John Adams	October 30, 1735; Braintree (Quincy), MA	Federalist	March 4, 1797 - March 4, 1801	July 4, 1826; Quincy, MA
Thomas Jefferson	April 13, 1743; Abermarle Cty., VA	Democratic-Republican	March 4, 1801 - March 4, 1809	July 4, 1826; Charlottesville, VA
James Madison	March 16, 1751; Port Conway, VA	Democratic-Republican	March 4, 1809 - March 4, 1817	June 28, 1836; Orange County, VA
James Monroe	April 28, 1758; Westmoreland Cty., VA	Democratic-Republican	March 4, 1817 - March 4, 1825	July 4, 1831; New York, NY
John Quincy Adams	July 11, 1767; Braintree (Quincy), MA	Democratic-Republican	March 4, 1825 - March 4, 1829	February 23, 1848; Washington, D.C
Andrew Jackson	March 15, 1767; Waxhaw, SC	Democratic	March 4, 1829 - March 4, 1837	June 8, 1845; Nashville, TN
Martin Van Buren	December 5, 1782; Kinderhook, NY	Democratic	March 4, 1837 - March 4, 1841	July 24, 1862; Kinderhook, NY
William Henry Harrison	February 9, 1773; Berkeley, VA	Whig	March 4, 1841 - April 4, 1841	April 4, 1841; Washington, D.C.
John Tyler	March 29, 1790; Charles City Cty., VA	Whig	April 4, 1841 - March 4, 1845	January 18, 1862; Richmond, VA
James Polk	November 2, 1795; Mecklenburg Cty., NC	Democratic	March 4, 1845 - March 4, 1849	June 15, 1849; Nashville, TN
Zachary Taylor	November 24, 1784; Orange Cty., VA	Whig	March 4, 1849 - July 9, 1850	July 9, 1850; Washington, D.C.
Millard Fillmore	January 7, 1800; Locke Township, NY	Whig	July 9, 1850 - March 4, 1853	March 8, 1874; Buffalo, NY
Franklin Pierce	November 23, 1804; Hillsborough, NH	Democratic	March 4, 1853 - March 4, 1857	October 8, 1869; Concord, NH
James Buchanan	April 23, 1791; Cove Gap, PA	Democratic	March 4, 1857 - March 4, 1861	June 1, 1868; Lancaster, PA
Abraham Lincoln	February 12, 1809; Hardin Cty., KY	Republican	March 4, 1861 - April 15, 1865	April 15, 1865; Washington, D.C.
Andrew Johnson	December 29, 1808; Raleigh, NC	Republican	April 15, 1865 - March 4, 1869	July 31, 1875; Carter County, TN
Ulysses S. Grant	April 27, 1822; Point Pleasant, OH	Republican	March 4, 1869 - March 4, 1877	July 23, 1885; Mount McGregor, NY
Rutherford B. Hayes	October 4, 1822; Delaware, OH	Republican	March 4, 1877 - March 4, 1881	January 17, 1893; Fremont, OH
James Garfield	November 18, 1831; Orange, OH	Republican	March 4, 1881 - September 19, 1881	September 19, 1881; Elberon, NJ
Chester Arthur	October 5, 1830; North Fairfield, VT	Republican	September 20, 1881 - March 4, 1885	November 18, 1886; New York, NY
Grover Cleveland	March 18, 1837; Caldwell, NJ	Democratic	March 4, 1885 - March 4, 1889; March 4, 1893 - March 4, 1897	June 24, 1908; Princeton, NJ

Presidents of the United States

President	Birth	Party	Term	Death
Benjamin Harrison	August 20, 1833; North Bend, OH	Republican	March 4, 1889 - March 4, 1893	March 13, 1901; Indianapolis, IN
William McKinley	January 29, 1843; Niles OH	Republican	March 4, 1897 - September 14, 1901	September 14, 1901; Buffalo, NY
Theodore Roosevelt	October 27, 1858; New York, NY	Republican	September 14, 1901 - March 4, 1909	January 6, 1919; Oyster Bay, NY
William H. Taft	September 15, 1857; Cincinnati, OH	Republican	March 4, 1909 - March 4, 1913	March 8, 1930; Washington, D.C.
Woodrow Wilson	December 28, 1856; Staunton, VA	Democratic	March 4, 1913 - March 4, 1921	February 3, 1924; Washington, D.C.
Warren Harding	November 2, 1865; Corsica, OH	Republican	March 4, 1921 - August 2, 1923	August 2, 1923; San Francisco, CA
Calvin Coolidge	July 4, 1872; Plymouth, VT	Republican	August 3, 1923 - March 4, 1929	January 5, 1933; Northampton, MA
Herbert Hoover	August 10, 1874; West Branch, IA	Republican	March 4, 1929 - March 4, 1933	October 20, 1964; New York, NY
Franklin D. Roosevelt	January 30, 1882; Hyde Park, NY	Democratic	March 4, 1933 - April 12, 1945	April 12, 1945; Warm Springs, GA
Harry S. Truman	May 8, 1884; Lamar, MO	Democratic	April 12, 1945 - January 20, 1953	December 26, 1972; Kansas City, MO
Dwight Eisenhower	October 14, 1890; Denison, TX	Republican	January 20, 1953 - January 20, 1961	March 28, 1969; Washington, D.C.
John F. Kennedy	May 29, 1917; Brookline, MA	Democratic	January 20, 1961 - November 22, 1963	November 22, 1963; Dallas, TX
Lyndon Johnson	August 27, 1908; Stonewall, TX	Democratic	November 22, 1963 - January 20, 1969	January 22, 1973; San Antonio, TX
Richard Nixon	January 9, 1913; Yorba Linda, CA	Republican	January 20, 1969 - August 9, 1974	April 22, 1994; New York, NY
Gerald Ford	July 14, 1913; Omaha, NE	Republican	August 9, 1974 - January 20, 1977	December 26, 2006; Rancho Mirage, CA
Jimmy Carter	October 1, 1924; Plains, GA	Democratic	January 20, 1977 - January 20, 1981	
Ronald Reagan	February 6, 1911; Tampico, IL	Republican	January 20, 1981 - January 20, 1989	June 5, 2004; Bel Air, CA
George H. W. Bush	June 12, 1924; Milton, MA	Republican	January 20, 1989 - January 20, 1993	
William J. Clinton	August 19, 1946; Hope, AR	Democratic	January 20, 1993 - January 20, 2001	
George W. Bush	July 6, 1946; New Haven, CT	Republican	January 20, 2001 - January 20, 2009	
Barack Obama	August 4, 1961 Honolulu, Hawaii	Democratic	January 20, 2009 -	

Index

A
Allies, 12, 18
Antiwar movement, 47
Apollo spacecrafts, 53
Armstrong, Neil, 9, 53, 59
atomic weapons, 6, 14, 30
Axis powers, 12

B
Bay of Pigs, 28
Berlin Wall, 29
blockade, 28, 29, 30
boycott, 17, 30, 31
Brown v. Board of Education of, 8, 18, 31
business, 14, 36, 40, 41, 50

C
cabinet, 3, 14, 54-55
Castro, Fidel, 20, 28, 33
China, 6
Civil Rights Act (1957), 18, 37
Civil Rights Act (1964), 39, 43, 59
Civil Rights Movement, 8, 31
Cold War, 4, 16
Communism, 4, 13, 18, 26
Congress, U.S., 14, 18, 28, 31, 39, 40, 41, 42, 44, 56, 57
Congress of Racial Equality, 31
Connally, John, 32
Constitution, U.S., 20, 31, 56
counterculture, 9
Cuba, 9, 20, 28, 29, 30, 33, 59

D
D Day, 12
Democrat, 10, 13, 14, 18, 24, 25, 32, 37, 38, 42, 44, 49, 60-61
desegregation, 41, 59
Diem, Ngo Ninh, 30
Durkin, Martin, 14, 54

E
Egypt, 18, 59
Eisenhower, Dwight, 3, 4, 10-21, 22, 24, 26, 37, 50, 59, 61
    born, 10, 61
    died, 10, 21, 61
    First Lady, 10, 15
    term, 10, 18, 61
    vice president, 10, 17, 21, 54
Eisenhower, Mary "Mamie" Doud, 10, 15
Eisenhower Doctrine, 18, 20
elections, presidential,
    of 1952, 10, 13
    of 1956, 17-18, 24
    of 1960, 7, 26, 38, 43
    of 1964, 27, 32, 40, 42
    of 1968, 43, 47, 49
electoral,
    College, 26
    map, 26
    vote(s), 26
Explorer spacecraft, 52, 59

F
Faubus, Orval, 18, 20
federal, 18, 30, 41, 59
Fitzgerald, "Honey", 24
France, 12, 27
Freedom Rides, 31

G
Gagarin, Yuri, 52
Gemini spacecraft, 52
gentleman's agreements, 8, 9
Germany, 9, 12, 27, 42
Glenn, John, 52
Goldwater, Barry, 42, 44
Great Britain, 12, 30, 56
"Great Society", 44
Gulf of Tonkin Resolution, 42

H
Head Start Program, 40, 44
Highway Beautification Act, 41
hippies culture, 9
House Un-American Activities, 8
    Committee,
Humphrey, Hubert H., 25, 34, 42, 43, 49, 55
Hungary, 18
hydrogen bomb (H-bomb), 6

I
Indochina, 16
Italy, 12

J
Japan, 6, 12, 36
Job Corps, 44
Johnson, Claudia "Lady Bird", 40
Johnson, Lyndon, 3, 4, 22, 33, 34-49, 53, 54, 59, 61
    born, 34, 61
    died, 34, 49, 61
    First Lady, 34, 40
    term, 34, 61
    vice president, 34, 42, 43, 55
Johnson, Sam Ealy, 34
Johnson treatment, 37

K
Kefauver, Estes, 7, 18, 24
Kennedy, Jacqueline Bouvier, 27, 28
Kennedy, John F., 3, 7, 18, 22-33, 34, 38, 43, 47, 50, 59, 61
    born, 22, 24, 61
    died, 22, 32, 61
    First Lady, 22, 27
    term, 22, 61
    vice president, 22, 25, 54
Kennedy, Joseph, 24
Kennedy, Robert F., 47, 50, 54, 55
Khrushchev, Nikita, 29
King, Martin Luther Jr., 8, 30, 31, 45, 48, 50, 59
Kleberg, Richard, 36
Korea, 6, 14, 16

L
Lebanon, 20
Leonov, Alexei, 52
Little Rock Central High, 20
Lodge, Henry Cabot, 24, 26

M
MacArthur Douglas, 10
Maddox, the, 42
Mao Zedong, 6
March on Washington, 30, 31
Marines, U.S., 46
Marshall, George, 12
Marshall, Thurgood, 45
McCarthy Eugene, 47
McCarthy, Joseph, 8, 13, 16, 17
McCarthyism, 16, 17
Medicare, 44
Mercury 6 spacecraft, 52
Miller, William, 42
Montgomery Bus Boycott, 31

N
National Aeronautics and Space, 9, 20, 59
    Administration (NASA),

Index

National Association for the, 31
    Advancement of Colored
    People,
    NAACP,
National Youth Administration, 36
new frontier, 25, 28
Nixon, Richard, 7, 10, 12, 13, 17,
    18, 21, 24, 26, 49, 54, 59, 61
North Atlantic Treaty Organization,
    12
    (NATO),
North Korea, 6
Nuclear Test-Ban Treaty, 30

O

Onassis, Aristotle, 27
Oswald, Lee Harvey, 33

P

Parks, Rosa, 17
Peace Corps, 28
polio, 9, 19
primary, 48
Profiles in Courage, 24

R

Rayburn, Sam, 37
Red Scare, 8
Republican, 7, 8, 10,12, 13, 14, 18,
    24, 26, 32, 37, 42, 49, 60, 61
Roosevelt, Eleanor, 41
Roosevelt, Franklin D., 10, 14, 36,
    58, 61
Ruby, Jack, 33

S

Salk, Jonas, 19
segregation, 8, 9, 17, 18, 30, 31
Southern Christian Leadership
    Conference, 31
South Korea, 6
Soviet Union, 4, 12, 15, 16, 20, 30,
    52, 59
space race, 20, 52
Sparkman, John, 13
Sputnik spacecraft, 20, 52, 59
Stalin, Joseph, 16
Stevenson, Adlai, 13, 18, 24
subversives, 8, 9
Supreme Court, 8, 17, 18, 20, 31,
    33, 45, 59
Suez Canal, 18

T

telecommunications, 9
television, 7, 8, 9, 13, 17, 26, 32,
    33, 53
Texas Broadcasting Corporation, 40
Truman, Harry S., 10, 12, 13, 14,
    58, 61
Twenty-Second Amendment, 20

V

Vietnam, 7, 9, 16, 30, 41, 42, 43,
    45, 46, 47, 48, 49, 50, 53, 59
Voting Rights Act, 44

W

warmonger, 42, 43
Warren, Earl, 33
Warren Report, 33
White, Ed, 52
White House, 14, 15, 18, 20, 21,
    22, 27, 33, 41, 49, 50, 53
World War II, 4, 6, 12, 22, 24, 30,
    40, 58

Further Reading

Aronson, Marc. *Robert Kennedy (Up Close Series)*. Penguin Group (USA), 2008.

Bausum, Ann. *Our Country's Presidents*. National Geographic Children's Books, 2009.

De Capua, Sarah. *Vietnam Memorial*. Children's Press (CT), 2008.

Hansen, Sarah. *Dwight D. Eisenhower*. The Child's World, Inc., 2008.

Harper, Judith. *John F. Kennedy*. The Child's World, Inc., 2008.

Maupin, Melissa. *Lyndon Baines Johnson*. The Child's World, Inc., 2008.

Pastan, Amy. *Eyewitness First Ladies*. DK Publishing, 2008.

Rodhe, Paul and Beatrice, Paul. *Kids Meet the Presidents*. Cider Mill Press Book Publishers, LLC, 2009.

Rubel, David. *Encyclopedia of the Presidents and Their Times*. Scholastic, Inc., 2009.

Wiest, Andrew. *The Vietnam War*. The Rosen Publishing Group Inc., 2008.

Websites to Visit

www.enchantedlearning.com/history/us/pres/list.shtml

www.whitehouse.gov/kids

pbskids.org/wayback

www.kidsinfo.com/American_History/Presidents.html